THE KISTE AND OGAN SOCIAL CHANGE
SERIES IN ANTHROPOLOGY

Editors

ROBERT C. KISTE   EUGENE OGAN

University of Minnesota

James L. Peacock was born in Montgomery, Alabama. He
received his undergraduate degree at Duke University
and received his Ph.D. at Harvard University. His
specialization is social anthropology. He has done
most of his field work in Southeast Asia and southeast
United States. Dr. Peacock was a member of the
Executive Board of American Anthropological Association
from 1975 to 1978. Currently, he is Professor and
Chairman of the Department of Anthropology at the
University of North Carolina at Chapel Hill.

THE MUHAMMADIJAH MOVEMENT
IN INDONESIAN ISLAM

 The Benjamin/Cummings Publishing Company

PURIFYING THE FAITH

JAMES L. PEACOCK

*University of North Carolina
at Chapel Hill*

Menlo Park, California

*Cover Photo. K.H.A. Dahlan, the founder of
the Muhammadijah Movement.*

*The Benjamin/Cummings Publishing Company
2727 Sand Hill Road
Menlo Park, California 94025*

Contents

Illustrations

Foreword

Dr. James Peacock's study is the eighth volume in the present series of ethnographic case studies on social and cultural change. No human group today, with the possible exception of a few small populations in the most remote regions of the earth, remains unaffected by other peoples and current world events. The studies comprising this series reflect this basic state of the human condition in the latter part of the twentieth century, and they focus on a common theme: the ways in which members of contemporary societies respond to, and develop strategies for coping with, modifications of their social and/or physical environments. Each study in the series is based on original field research by the author.

Dr. Peacock's contribution to this series addresses the subject of change on at least three levels. His specific concern is change within a major religious tradition—Islam— as that change is accomplished in the relatively recently independent nation of Indonesia. At this level, the book addresses the general problem of the impulse to reform social and cultural institutions.

Drawing on his years of research in Indonesia, Peacock is further able to place the Muhammadijah reform movement in the context of the vast changes which have taken place in Indonesia from the years of the great kingdoms, through colonization, war and independence struggles, to the present. Here, in admirably concise summary, he provides the reader with an idea of what macrocosmic social change has meant in this part of the world.

At the third level, Peacock indicates how the Muhammadijah movement itself has been affected by and, in turn, shapes change taking place in larger Indonesian society. Whether in terms of electoral politics, economic modernization, or changing conceptions of women's roles in society, Muhammadijah both reflects and provides new directions for this complex nation-state.

There are two other features of Peacock's book which seem to us distinctive. One is his examination of the biography of the movement's leader. He sketches the theoretical arguments of the sociologist Max Weber and the psychologist Erik Erikson about such leadership, and shows how they may apply in this specific case.

The other is his "ethnographic diary" approach. In personalized descriptions of his own participant observations as he travels around movement centers and lives with Muhammadijah members in an indoctrination camp, Peacock gives students (who constitute the primary audience for this series) a real feel for what it is like to be an ethnographer in a particular field situation.

The book thus can be read by those with varied interests. It adds material on Southeast Asia to the series. Like Miller's *Old Villages and a New Town*, it deals with a modernizing society; like Tonkinson's *The Jigalong Mob*, it increases our understanding of different religions. And it illustrates clearly just how complex the subject of social and cultural change may be.

University of Minnesota   ROBERT C. KISTE

Minneapolis, Minnesota   EUGENE OGAN

Series Editors

Preface

I met Professor James L. Peacock and got acquainted with
him in 1970 when he was busy studying about Muhammadijah, its
ideal, development, and activities. Holding a notebook in
one hand and a pencil in the other, he talked to people, to
Muhammadijah leaders and to its youth, in his smooth and
fluent Indonesian. He distributed questionnaires. He found
himself amidst the participants of what is called Darol-Arqom
or—in common term—a training center. He visited Muhammadijah schools, hospitals, orphanages, mosques, courses, and
meetings. His pencil was moving rapidly across the blank
sheet as he listened and watched. It seemed that not a thing
could escape him unnoticed.

As an organization Muhammadijah has proved itself not only
to be an educational and social movement but also a reformist
movement that has created the great awakening of the Indonesian Moslems which is now still in progress. It was only
three years after the Japanese had defeated the Russians at
the battle of Manchuria in 1905, when a certain Indonesian
physician by the name of Wahidin Soedirohoesodo founded an
organization named Budi Utomo. In 1911, the Sarekat Dagang
Islam was formed by Haji Samanhoedi, and in the same year an
ulama or Islamic scholar opened a private school bearing the
name of "Muhammadijah." On November 18 the following year,
he founded an organization under the same name. While Budi
Utomo seemed to be intended apparently for the middle-class
and the Sarekat Dagang Islam was founded for joining together
the Moslem Batik Producers in their struggle against Chinese
commercial domination, Muhammadijah was able to unite the
mass in general. In 1912, the Sarekat Dagang Islam changed
into a political party named Sarekat Islam.

Muhammadijah soon spread widely, moving and operating in the field of Islamic propagation, education, and social affairs. But above all, the organization teaches that Islam not merely preaches the religious rituals, but also calls and guides its followers to promote the condition of human societies in every aspect of life. Muhammadijah has taught the people and laid bare what the religion of Islam really is. Islam has for ages been covered by ignorance, cults, mysticism, and superstitious beliefs that made the Islamic peoples easy prey to colonialism. Muhammadijah endeavours to disclose the real Islam as Jamaluddin and Abduh did. To some extent the attempt has been successful. The disclosure has been formulated and stated as the aim of the movement in the statute of Muhammadijah which runs: "To uphold and to uplift the teachings of Islam so as to create the true Islamic society."

Unlike other writers who are focusing their attention mainly on the educational and social activities of Muhammadijah, Professor James L. Peacock has busied himself commenting on and analyzing the ideal, ideology, and mental attitude of its leaders and even their personalities. He deals with Muhammadijah as a mass-organization or, to be more exact, as a living thing. He describes the condition of the cultural ground on which Muhammadijah has come to life and developed. He tells us how the Muhammadijah leaders interpret the doctrines of Islam. He shows the democratic sphere between leaders and members. In doing so, his work becomes more vivid and colourful.

This present work is no doubt of great value and most useful not only to those who are eager to learn more about Muhammadijah but also to anyone who is interested in the development of the Islamic people in Indonesia and its surroundings, which in the years to come will probably emerge as a potential power.

Hereby, therefore feeling greatly honoured, I present this very work of Professor James L. Peacock to the reader.

Jogjakarta, September, 1975

DJARNAWI HADIKUSUMA
Secretary-General of the Central
Leadership of Muhammadijah
with the consent of
Mr. A. R. Fakhruddin
the President.

Acknowledgements

For funds which made possible the field and library research
on which this study is based, I gratefully acknowledge the aid
of the National Science Foundation, the American Council of
Learned Societies, the Wenner Gren Foundation for Anthropological Research, and the Research Council of the University
of North Carolina. For sponsorship, I thank L.I.P.I., the
Indonesian Science Foundation. For helpful editorial sugges-
tions I thank especially Dr. Eugene Ogan, and for research
assistance Mr. Brett Sutton. For careful checking of factual
materials concerning the Muhammadijah I am most grateful to
the former head of the Indonesian Muslim Party, Djarnawi
Hadikusuma, and the Minister of Religion of the Republic of
Indonesia, Professor Mukti Ali. Mr. Djarnawi Hadikusuma
kindly contributed a Preface to this study, which is repro-
duced here in the excellent and charming English in which he
wrote it; it is not a translation. I am particularly grateful to Mr. Djarnawi for this effort, which is of great value
and properly expresses the participant's view of what the
anthropologist has reported about that in which he partici-
pates—his movement and his culture.

J. L. P.

CHAPTER ONE

Introduction: Movements and Cultural Meaning

"Sire, the peasants are revolting," said the minister to the
king. "Yes, aren't they," replied the king as he grimaced in
distaste. Thus we laugh at (and secretly empathize with) a
conservatism which we suppose to have been the attitude of
feudal royalty and imagine as existing today perhaps only
among overstuffed gentlemen in British clubs or in cartoons of
the *New Yorker*. Such conservatism or traditionalism, which is
also elitism, goes against the grain of a democratic society
and is mistrusted. A more folksy type of traditionalism, that
of the "natural man," the pioneer, mountaineer, or dirt farmer
is more easily appreciated, at least among the young and the
disaffected, and such a life-style has gained new publicity
through country music and the back-to-the-earth movement.
But note the term *movement*. Even regaining tradition becomes
a campaign, a revolt, a reform movement. Our efforts at
traditionalism express the fundamental and underlying value
of our society, which is reformism. Fundamentally we assume
that everyone should contribute, should "do something," and
that what they should do is make things better, i.e., reform.
The results range from tax reform to women's and minorities'
movements and even, paradoxically, reform movements which endeavor to restore traditionalism. Most of us would find it
difficult to imagine ourselves living in a society where reform is not a central value.

Yet human history, stretching back a half-million years, is
dominated more by a sense of tradition than of reform.
Reformism has come to the forefront only in the past four centuries. Prior to the modern epoch, and still in some places,
normal people felt that their fundamental obligation was not

to make things better, but to uphold tradition. Such traditions were conceived not so much as ways of the past but as received culture which, though in fact it might be in constant flux, had always been and always would be; in the word of the Australian aborigine, such a tradition exists in *everywhen*. The traditions that one should uphold ranged from tribal rules governing relations among kin to Confucian prescriptions for the behavior of government officials. The point is not that no one ever saw the need for changing such traditions or tried to do so, but rather that for most people the most fundamental value, the obligation central to one's life, was not to change their received culture but to perpetuate it. If this generalization is true, and it would seem grossly so, then the basic thrust of our modern society veers sharply from the basic orientation of most societies in human history. Our itch to constantly improve, to reform, is unusual indeed, rather peculiar and perhaps even pathological in some circumstances. How did we get this itch? While economic, political, and geographical factors can be cited, a basic source is our recent cultural history. We ourselves spring from a reformation movement.

The largest world religions—Islam, Christianity, and Buddhism—all originated as reformation movements. All evolved, during the period 500 B.C. to 600 A.D., as efforts to purify the faith. In a Hinduist society that identified rebirth with the worldly order of castes, Buddhism created an otherworldly civilization of monks and meditation; Islam's holy war and monotheistic ethic cut through a desert religion of tribes and patrimonies; and Christianity worked against mystery cults and forest spirits to elevate an ideal of the spiritual life based on the sacrifice of a savior. In its own way, each of these world religions strove to purge existence of a tangle of social establishments embedded in spirits, cults, and idols, and to create a purer way, a path based on a radical commitment to the ultimate.

The drive to purity gave impetus to evangelism. These movements attracted many believers, and they spread widely —Buddhism throughout Asia, Islam from Africa to Indonesia, and Christianity in the West. With spread came dilution, mixture, and bureaucratization. The pure faith became vast empires, ecclesiastical bureaucracies, cults, fetishes, magical practices, and scholastic elaboration of the holy texts.

These accretions came to be seen as a pollution of the pure, and there erupted movements to purify, to reform. Such movements have been especially frequent during the past four hundred years, that is, in modern history. Most familiar to Westerners, of course, is the Protestant Reformation which signaled the end of the Middle Ages in the West. On the

religious plane, the Protestant Reformation called for the
purge of ceremony, the flattening of hierarchy, the cleansing
of the world of magic, saints, and fetishes, reliance on the
word of the original scripture, and the clearing of the chan-
nel between man and God. These religious reforms were associated with profound transformations of Western culture, society, and psychology. Values became more individualistic,
society became more democratic, and everyone was responsible
for his own salvation, which was assured by an ascetic, lifelong, methodically-planned struggle to prove his fitness for
eternal life. This so-called Protestant Ethic came to influence such diverse spheres as business, science, education,
and the family, and it still determines our culture's values
and way of life.

Buddhism, too, has its reform movements, but, on the whole,
these appear to have had less secular impact than did the
Protestant Reformation; the other-worldliness of Buddhism
perhaps encouraged the containing of the reformist impulse
within the monkhood and certain sects, inhibiting spillage
into the wider society. What about Islam?

The modern reformation movement in Islam began in central
Arabia in 1744 when a certain Mohammed ibn Abd al-Wahhab
initiated a radical and militant campaign that came to be
known as the Wahhabi. The Wahhabis condemned the saint worship and mystic exercises of the Sufis, and they exhorted a
return to the pure faith of strict monotheism. For their
cause, they took up arms. They were defeated, though not
before capturing and "purifying" Mecca, but military defeat
did not kill the cultural impulse. Reformist ideas were tak-
en up by Islamic movements in the Middle East, in India, and
in Northern Africa. Reformist doctrine culminated in the
formulations of Egypt's Muhammed Abduh at the turn of the
twentieth century.

The tenets of Islamic reformism resemble those of Christian
Protestantism. The reformists preach scripturalism—a reliance on the Qur'an instead of the hierarchy of officials or
the commentaries of scholars; the simplification of ceremony;
and the purge of saint and spirit worship, and of any other
idolatry which distracts from allegiance to the one God. The
reformists also moved to modernize the culture and the society; they founded schools and youth and women's organizations.
(In patriarchial Islam, the issue of emancipation of women has
been rather a bump on the smooth highway of modernization.)
Whether the Islamic reformation has had the cultural, social,
and psychological impact as profound as that claimed for the
Protestant Ethic is subject to debate, but certainly the
Islamic reformation is among the factors that set the stage
for the contemporary resurgence and renaissance of the Islamic
world.

The question of the impact of Islam and its reformation in
Southeast Asia is especially intriguing. Southeast Asia is
far removed, both geographically and culturally, from the
Semitic heartland and North African borderlands that have been
hospitable to Islam and its reformist impulse. In contrast to
the arid and harsh deserts and mountains of the Arab world,
Southeast Asia is a lush, humid, tropical garden. And in contrast to the Arab ethic of manliness, aggression, and conflict,
Southeast Asian culture is a tapestry of willowy dancers,
courtly manners, poetic language, and cosmologies and community values emphasizing tranquility and harmony. Could the
harsh and purist ethic of Islamic reformism take hold in such
a milieu? And if so, with what effect—destruction, dynamism,
chaos, or what?

A circumstantial and circumscribed answer to this query and
the larger one on the meaning of reformation is provided by
perusal of a single Islamic reformation movement in Southeast
Asia, the Muhammadijah of Indonesia. Boasting millions of
members and covering thousands of miles of island territory,
Muhammadijah is certainly the most powerful living reformist
movement in Muslim Southeast Asia, perhaps in the entire Muslim culture. In its own homeland of Indonesia, which is the
fifth largest nation in the world, Muhammadijah is one of the
three or four most important social, religious, and educational movements. The career of Muhammadijah, which we shall
examine after consideration of some general issues, is remarkable. This movement has provided a cause, an order, a
meaning for people whose culture, for all its subtlety and
richness, has experienced in recent history the most disturbing and destructive forces of change.

Why Study Movements? Movements evoke distinctive methods
of study. The study of change in the overall pattern of a
society requires the sampling and synthesis of diverse data.
Signs of change in diverse sectors—economic, political, religious, educational—and various regions and classes must somehow be sampled and summarized. Given the range of data, a
likely technique is the statistical. Thus, public-opinion
polls endeavor to sample attitudes or opinions of varied
strata of a society and to summarize patterns and trends
through counting and comparing the various responses. Occasionally an analyst will synthesize a great number of such
polls to hazard conclusions about the change or lack of it in
the overall pattern of society.

Movements have, in a way, done the sampling and synthesis
for the investigator. Bounded and discrete, movements express—simply, idealistically, emphatically—issues which are
basic but unarticulated in the larger society. Consider what
Feminism and Martin Luther King, Jr., have achieved in artic-

ulating those conflicts and potentialities for relations between the sexes and between the races that are latent in the
life of society as a whole. When sleeping dogs wake and stand
up, they are seen. Approached sensitively, with awareness of
their biases, movements highlight for us themes fundamental to
the workings of the wider system.

For social anthropology, movements provide a particularly
congenial way into the study of complex society. Social anthropology is traditionally designed for the study of small
communities, such as the tribal or peasant village. In the
small community, many facets of life—political, economic,
educational, religious, aesthetic—are concentrated in a limited arena, a small theater whose activities can be observed
directly by a single investigator. In contrast, the vast
workings of a complex society can never be directly observed
by an investigator; to watch all of the economic or religious
activities of all Americans is impossible, even if one devoted a lifetime to such a task. The study of overall trends
and patterns in a complex society requires much selection
and abstraction—the type of sampling and statistical analysis
mentioned above, for example. A movement is, however, in
many respects like a small village. It concentrates a range
of activities within a single, bounded unit. Movements, insofar as they become involving, encompass myriad aspects of
their members' lives—domestic, political, religious, aesthetic; think of Nazism and Communism, or, for that matter, of
Feminism. Further, movements typically bring together these
various themes in meetings: rallies, ceremonies, marches,
and camps. These gatherings can be observed first-hand,
directly, and in a fairly short time by social anthropologists,
much as they were accustomed through the classical *participant observation* to study the small community. Here their
small unit of observation, however, is assumed to express
trends and forces of the wider, complex society.

Reformation Movements

Movements can be classified in many ways. One of the sim-
plest ways is by asking what aspect of existence the movement
desires to change. The classification will be arbitrary, of
course, since movements tend to draw together myriad aspects
of existence. Rough distinctions can nonetheless be made.
Thus, political movements, such as nationalist, Communist, or
secessionist, are concerned with changing the structure of
government. Social movements, such as those of labor, women,
and minorities, are concerned with changing basic conditions
and laws of society. Psychological movements, such as psy-
choanalysis or Transcendental Meditation, Subud, and other

endeavors at mystical meditation wish to change aspects of
the self. Ecological movements, such as the Whole Earth, desire to change the relation of humans to their environment.

Following this line of distinctions, reformation movements
are concerned with changing a system of religion. Such reform usually calls for a simplification of current practice
in order to return to the uncorrupted condition of the system at the time of its origin. In the reformations of Islam
and Christianity, for example, ritual is to be streamlined,
the hierarchy of priests or officials is to be eliminated,
and truth is to be sought not from the elaborate interpretations of authorities but directly from the scripture itself.
The desired result will be a purified religion, one like that
originally established by Muhammad or Christ.

The reforms espoused often appear trivial to the outsider,
and one wonders why they generate so much dispute. What
difference does it make, in Islam, whether one gauges the
start of the month of fast by astronomical calculations or by
looking at the moon? Why does it matter whether one does a
certain prayer six times instead of ten? To the outsider,
reformists may seem legalistic and obsessive in their concern
to scrub away each superstition, each ritual increment, each
practice that has become custom but is not part of the original, the true design of the founder.

The reason for the reformist's concern lies in the character of the religious system. For those who believe, religions
serve to define the ultimate meaning of existence. A religion
delineates symbols, values, and beliefs that define the world
as meaningful, that subsume under these categories those
events and objects of existence that would otherwise be left
naked and meaningless. Any element in the religion thus as-
sumes meaning for the believer beyond that apparent to the
outsider. Such an element, for the believer, is not merely a
genuflection, a wafer, or two crossed sticks, but it is a
category which is part of a scheme that bestows meaning.
Owing to their place in the systems, such categories are sacred. They define orientations cutting deeply into life, and
to change them is deeply disorienting. Accordingly, the
prospect of change, as in reformation, provokes the faithful
to brutal resistence, the reformist to fanatical wars, and
all believers to the most painful and disturbing reflection
on self and surroundings.

Models for the Study of Reformation Movements

Of the diverse studies of reformation, two stand out as
classic and as particularly relevant to the case to be ana-
lyzed here. The first is the socio-cultural analysis of

Calvinism by the sociologist Max Weber (1958). The second is
the psycho-historical analysis of Luther by the psychologist
Erik Erikson (1958). Both treat the Protestant Reformation
within Christianity.

   Weber's classical work, *The Protestant Ethic and the Spirit
of Capitalism,* emphasized the Puritanism that grew out of the
reformation of John Calvin. Calvinist doctrine sharply distinguished those who would be saved from those who would eter-
nally suffer in Hell; the elect were differentiated from the
damned. According to Calvin, God has predestined each person
to be one or the other. The Calvinist was understandably concerned to assure himself that he was of the elect. As Calvinist theology evolved, the primary mode of assurance became
that of action: to act as though one were saved by laboring
as though one were a saint—called to work for the glory of
God. In Weber's view, this impetus toward service for God
came to influence all of life. The Calvinist rationalized
life into a focused, relentless, continuous labor for God.
Out of this motive grew the Spirit of Capitalism, which was
a work ethic in secular life that mirrored the Protestant
Ethic in religion.

   Treating movements in general, Weber (1947, pp. 324-367)
distinguished three phases: traditional, charismatic, and
bureaucratic. The traditional phase is marked by adherence
to such stable bases of authority as leaders and norms of
tribe and patrimony. The charismatic phase shifts allegiance
to the charismatic leader. Where in traditionalism, authority
is vested in the group and its norms, the charismatic movement vests authority in the unique spiritual qualities of the
leader; as Jesus said, *I* am the way. The trademark of charismatic movements is enthusiasm. Reacting vigorously against
traditional values and structures, the charismatic leader
proclaims a new vision. Followers are caught in ecstatic
trances, fits, and other expressions of unleashed emotion.
In time, the charismatic leader declines and dies. If the
movement endures, the leader is replaced by others, usually
more than one. The multiple functions that the founder em-
braced in person become differentiated into various divisions
of the movement. Each division acquires offices and officers,
and the movement becomes a bureaucracy. Sect becomes church;
nationalism, nation.

   From Weber, one learns of three types of rationalization as
part of movements. First, the belief system becomes rationalized in order to solve such fundamental problems of meaning
as: Will I be saved? Second, the organization of the movement becomes rationalized, as it evolves from charisma to
bureaucracy. Third, the conduct of life becomes rationalized
in order to more efficiently carry out the dictates of the
creed. The first level concerns the rationalization of

thought: the forging of ideas into a coherent and logical structure. The second and third types concern the rationalization of action: the organizing of collective and personal endeavors to methodically achieve goals of the movement.

Erikson treats Luther instead of Calvinism, that is, a man rather than a movement. In his *Young Man Luther*, Erikson (1958) probes the irrationalities of the inner life of the founder rather than the rationalization of the cultural and social aspects of the movement. Erikson's materials are biographical rather than sociological. For Weber's focus, Calvinism was the appropriate case; for Erikson's, Luther. Taken together, Erikson's and Weber's analyses yield a rounded perspective on reformation movements.

Erikson's argument, much simplified, is that Luther suffered from a tortured sense of guilt as part of his relations with his father, Hans Lueder; that he worked through this personal guilt at a spiritual level; that the result was his theological doctrine of justification by faith; and that this solution freed Luther of a neurotic youth and launched him on a vigorous reformation movement.

In the course of his analysis, Erikson employs concepts central to his other writings on psycho-history: the movement as a creative formulation growing out of tortured familial situations; the moratorium, or neurotic withdrawal and search within, that the charismatic reformer typically passes through en route to reformation; and the cultural formulation as personal solution.

Both Weber and Erikson have been criticized for their use of fact. The point in mentioning them here is not to embrace their empirical analyses but to acknowledge the inspiration of their studies as models. They not only interpret Calvinism and Luther but they also set forth a perspective which can be used in the study of other reformation movements. The case of interest here, which is the Muslim reformation movement, Muhammadijah, can be profitably viewed in some respects in terms of Weber's concept of the rationalization of doctrine, organization, and the conduct of life among its members. (The latter type of rationalization is treated in detail elsewhere [Peacock, 1978], while the focus here is on the movement.) An effort is made, also, to examine biographical materials of the founder of Muhammadijah, K. H. A. Dahlan, with an eye to the Eriksonian interpretation of the reformer. It turns out that certain configurations which Erikson found basic to Luther are absent in Dahlan; but then the comparison is suggestive.

The Ethnographic Approach

In one respect, the present study goes beyond the classical

perspectives of Weber and Erikson. The reformations they ex-
amined were dead, this one is alive. They were forced to rely
on historical documents. I was privileged to follow the method distinctive of ethnography, *participant observation*. The
first part of this case study is based on history and biography, but the latter part derives from my participant observation within the Muhammadijah movement from January to July,
1970. During this period, I took part in meetings, study
groups, conferences, and training camps—in short, the normal
round of activities of the movement—striving to gain a sense
of the aspirations, organization, and activities of the Muhammadijah.

In the Preface to this book, the head of the Indonesian Muslim Party, Djarnawi, deftly sketches a portrait of my role as
participant observer. He emphasizes that I took notes:
"Holding a notebook in one hand and a pencil in the other he
talked to people, to Muhammadijah leaders and to its youth....
His pencil was moving rapidly across the blank sheet as he
listened and watched." Djarnawi here emphasizes observation
over participation, though he alludes to that too. He exercises his excellent sense of humor to put me in my place—that
of observer, outsider.

Exactly how to define one's role as participant-observer is
a classic problem in ethnographic research. Traditionally one
is advised to seek a middle point between the extremes of the
fieldworker who goes native and the one who coldly stares at
the people as though they were specimens in a laboratory. This
issue of balancing observation and participation acquires a
new dimension in the study of movements. Movements tend toward
a radical view of outsiders; those who are not members are
enemies; those not for, are against. At the same time, movements desire converts. Thus movements do not easily set a
place for the neutral observer. The outsider tends to be regarded as either an enemy or a potential convert, or both.

Both attitudes entered my experience with the Muhammadijah,
though the Javanese sense of tact and moderation prevented
extremes in either direction. During the months of participation in the Muhammadijah, several efforts were made to win
my conversion to Islam. For example, a congregation of some
five hundred Muslims once prayed for several minutes that I
convert. More often, I experienced no direct pressure to convert—they realized that I was not the proper sheep for their
fold— but rather an effort to clarify my religious identity.

Christians (which is what I, as a Westerner, was generally
assumed to be) compete with Muslims for control of Indonesia,
and a certain conflict exists between the two movements. To
a degree, I could avoid the religious label by claiming to be
a scholar—one who learns as opposed to one who believes— but
the image of scholar too has been tainted. Muhammadijans used

the term *Orientalist* to refer to Western scholars (some of whom were employed by the Dutch during the colonial era) of Christian bias who studied Islam in order to denigrate or control it. Once at a large gathering of Muhammadijah teachers where I was attempting to explain my research, I was asked if I were such an Orientalist. I denied this, and someone in the assembled group then asked, "What, then, *is* your religion *(agama)*?" I replied, "My religion is Anthropology." The answer was doubtless cryptic and certainly idealistic, but I went on to explain that I was trying to follow an academic discipline, to acquire knowledge, to take notes. No one could be a truly neutral observer, but in terms of my observations of the Muhammadijah I would try to fulfill the requirements of the ethnographic method and avoid the more blatant biases of a sectarian point of view.

The objective of this book is to give a brief ethnography of the Muhammadijah. No such account now exists, in any language. I hope to give a circumstantial picture of the history and pattern of the Muhammadijah as it relates to the social and cultural change of Islamic Southeast Asia, especially Indonesia and particularly Java. No exhaustive or technical account is intended. I shall describe several "slices of life" within the Muhammadijah by presenting and interpreting primary texts, written either by Muhammadijans themselves, by eyewitnesses (including an Orientalist), or by myself based on my fieldnotes. These texts include a biography of the founder of the movement, a description of an early meeting, a travelogue survey of the island branches, and detailed observation of a Muhammadijah training camp. Before turning to the Muhammadijah proper, a sketch is given of the broad thrust of relevant Indonesian history. Working through the interpretation of these data, the reader should acquire an elementary sense of method in cultural anthropology along with a basic knowledge of the life of the Muhammadijah.

CHAPTER TWO

Indonesia

Of the three thousand islands comprising the nation of Indonesia, five account for nine-tenths of the land area: Sumatra, Sulawesi, Indonesian Borneo (the central and southern portions of that island, known as Kalimantan), West New Guinea, and Java.[1] Of the approximately 120 million inhabitants of Indonesia, some 70 million live on Java, and of these over 50 million speak the Javanese language and identify themselves as ethnically Javanese. It is these Javanese, who live primarily in eastern and central Java, among whom the Muslim reformist movement Muhammadijah originated. Muhammadijah's founder was Javanese, its earliest history and national headquarters are in Java, my investigations were concentrated on Java, and the focus of this study will be on Muhammadijah in Java.

Muhammadijah has, however, spread throughout all the islands, from Indonesia's northwestern corner, in Sumatra, to its southwestern tip, in West New Guinea. A brief survey will be given later, by way of a travelogue, of the movement among these outer islands peoples.

Animism

To judge from scattered archaeological and ethnological information, the religious pattern of Indonesia around the time

---

[1] Details and sources that document points included in this chapter may be found in Peacock (1973). See Map 1, page 16 for locales.

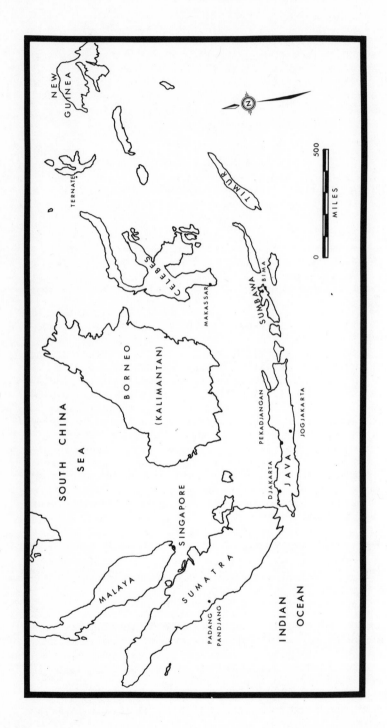

Map 1. Some Centers of Muhammadijah

of Christ was essentially animistic. Indonesians believed in
spirits which inhabited the universe and could become manifest
in any number of objects, persons, and places. A tree spirit,
a mountain spirit, or an ancestral spirit could evoke fear,
possess the unwary, and cause sickness, insanity, or death;
such a spirit could also elicit veneration and bring about
health, fertility, and happiness. To honor the good spirits,
placate the bad, and sustain a cosmic, psychic, and social order, a complex of rites was celebrated in connection with times
of planting and harvest, at birth, marriage, and death, and to
smooth sudden crises. The cosmos was conceived as an organized
structure of spiritual forces, sometimes divided into halves
such as male and female—a division that may have been associated with the division of society into halves of the type anthropologists term moieties.

Evidence concerning prehistoric Indonesia is skimpy, and we
do not know with any certainty what life was like then. A certain animism is still apparent today, however, even within a
highly sophisticated civilization such as that of the Javanese.
This animism is a major concern of such reformist movements as
the Muhammadijah.

Hinduization

Owing apparently to sea travel by Indonesians to the ports
of India, there was contact with the Hindus. During the early
centuries after the time of Christ, Hindu culture influenced
that of Indonesia. Hindu priests may have come to the early
Indonesian kingdoms, especially in Java, where they may have
been employed as chancellors, advisors in governmental affairs,
and supervisors of the construction of Hindu tombs, monuments,
and temples. During this period, it was believed that certain
Javanese rulers were the incarnation of Hindu gods, such as
Vishnu or Siva, and the propagation of such a belief may have
been the motive for Hinduization: by acquiring a mythical
sanctity, chiefs and minor rulers became great god-kings.
Whatever the dynamics, the spread of the Hindu religion was
associated with the florescence of great empires in Java and
their extension throughout the islands and even as far north
as mainland Southeast Asia. This period of Hinduized empires
lasted from the founding of the central Javanese kingdom,
Mataram, in the eighth century A.D., to the death gasp of the
east Javanese kingdom, Madjapahit, whose royalty fled to Bali
in the wake of a new Islamized Mataram that arose during the
seventeenth century A.D.

These Hindu-Javanese kingdoms displayed certain cultural
themes that interestingly compare with the archaic civiliza-
tions of India and China from which Java drew much influence.

As in China, the Javanese kingdoms centered around a state cult dependent on state officials, a gentlemanly aristocracy of bureaucrats whose philosophy was much like that of the Confucian mandarin. As in India, Javanese society was stratified, and it was believed that each stratum should obey its own distinct and separate code. Java also resembled India in its Hinduized tradition of mystical meditation: in remote forest schools, pupils learned ascetic techniques from a *guru* (teacher) whom they were supposed to esteem above their own fathers, and even kings withdrew into the forest for contemplation after the achievement of worldly deeds.

Despite these similarities to the Chinese and Indian models, Javanese civilization was quite distinct. It placed more emphasis on the god-king and the celestial kingdom. The Javanese king, known as Siva-Buddha, was an incarnation of the divine, a figure of stunning charisma who projected the blinding light of his divinity as a benevolent beam to protect his subjects. In rites, he would traverse his kingdom to mesh its contours with that of the cosmos, and the kingdom itself was designed to replicate the cosmos as conceived in Hindu-Buddhist-Javanese philosophy. The capital was oriented around the four cardinal points, and its holy pivot was symbolic of the cosmic Mount Meru: a palace that served as a repository for sacred objects which, if captured, signaled the fall of the empire.

Caste and notions of purity and pollution were not so important in Java as in India, but nevertheless the social order was hierarchical. The bureaucracy of the court was highly stratified, with elaborate systems of etiquette to order relations between the high and the low. Indeed, distinctions of status were elaborated into a vision of the universe such that high status was associated with spirituality, low status with the material, and this dichotomy extended into classifications of colors, substances, places, and other elements of life.

If the court was hierarchical and Hinduized, the village was communal and animistic. In the peasant village, land was jointly owned. Rights to dispose of that land were vested not in the individual but in the village council. The villagers' common bond to the land was celebrated by communal rites honoring the guardian spirit of the village. Agricultural rites, ceremonial feasts among neighbors, and charms and shrines to honor ghosts believed to hover around the village served to spiritually energize the community life.

Apart from the courts and village, the other major elements of archaic Javanese society were the hermitages and ports. These gave relief from the hierarchical and communal structures central to the established order. The hermitages in the forests and jungles housed communities of learned and holy teachers who were revered even by kings but who remained aloof

from the courts. The ports were based less on tribute from
inland peasants than on the taxing of seafaring merchants.
Coastal society was generally more egalitarian and open than
courtly society. Light literature—romantic, anecdotal, and
erotic—replaced the refined, spiritualized shadow plays, ceremonial dances, and percussion orchestras of the courts. The
coastal breezes blew fresh air toward the inland society, and
it was the relatively egalitarian ports that would serve as a
base for the spread of Islam.

Islamization

During the period of the great Hinduized kingdoms, trade
was gradually expanding along the sea routes of the islands of
Southeast Asia. By the thirteenth century A.D., the Far East,
Southeast Asia, India, Western Asia, and the Mediterranean had
become part of a trade network manned by Arabs, Persians, In-
dians, Chinese, Malays, and Indonesians. By 1400, the Hinduized Javanese kingdom of Madjapahit had extended its trade
into Timur, the Moluccas, and the Phillipines, and had stimulated the rise of ports along the north coast of Java.

Along these routes came Muslim traders, at first from the
Near East and India, then, as they converted the natives, from
Malaya and Indonesia itself. Missionaries as well as merchants,
the Muslim traders spread the faith throughout the Malayo-
Indonesian region. By the end of the thirteenth century A.D.
there existed scattered enclaves of Muslims on such islands as
Sumatra. During the fourteenth, fifteenth, sixteenth, and
seventeenth centuries, the islands were inundated by a kind of
Islamic tidal wave, resulting in the conversion of numerous
ports, in Java, Celebes, Sumbawa, the Moluccas, and elsewhere.

An important motive for conversion of the ports was economic.
Harbor kings who became Muslim enhanced the appeal of their
ports to taxable Muslim merchants. Islam was attractive, too,
because of its mysticism and magic—qualities appealing to the
Indonesians owning to their heritage of Hinduism and animism.
The earliest Muslims in the islands were of the mystical sect,
the Sufi. Teaching chants and exercises that achieve ecstatic
union with the divine and claiming new skills to manipulate
the spirits, these teachers were graciously received by kings
and given sacral status by the people. Moving inland, they
converted the Hinduist hermitages to Muslim schools, known as
pondok and *pesantren*—institutions which constituted the most
extensive system of public education for Indonesians from
1600 until 1945. Centered around the *pondok* and *pesantren*
there emerged in Indonesia a purist type of Muslim sometimes
known as the *santri* after the name for the student who studied
at the *pesantren*.

The Santri (Purist) Pattern. Rising at dawn, cooking his simple breakfast of rice over a flame, laboring in the fields by day, and practicing mysticism and such ascetic exercises as Javanese karate by night, the *santri* was guided by his teacher, the *kijai* who replaced the old Hinduist *guru*. Toward the *kijai*, as toward the *guru*, the student should feel complete devotion, indeed, a mystical bond. Yet the student did not confine himself to one teacher. During his adolescence and youth, he would wander through the wilderness from one school and teacher to another, mastering the scriptures that were the specialty of each. Eventually he might travel to Mecca. After study there with a master, he could return and establish his own school.

Religious life among the adult *santri* centered around the mosque and small houses of prayer. In these places, the predominantly male congregations would practice their five daily prayers, meet on Fridays for a sermon, and sometimes recite mystical dirges at night. Officers of the mosque, paid by the people, included the caller to prayer, the leader of prayer, and the preacher of sermons. In the stifling tropics, the mosque with its refreshing bath and cool tile floor was, for men, a welcome place of relief from daily labor, and it served as a social center, a men's house, as well as a place of worship.

Santri is the term used in Java for those persons who endeavor to faithfully practice the five pillars of Islam: the commitment to the faith ("There is no God but Allah and Muhammad is his Prophet"), the five daily prayers, the payment of a yearly tithe, the fast during Ramadan, and the pilgrimage to Mecca. In accord with the Near Eastern origins of Islam, the *santri* also adopt a quasi-Near Eastern style of life. They enjoy Near Eastern music, dance and poetry, they study the Arabic language, they read and write histories, epics, and biographies centered around figures of the Near East, and some adopt Arabic-like clothing and manner. While some of them have Arabic blood and resemble Arabs in appearance, the majority are genetically Malayo-Indonesian.

The Abangan (Syncretic) Pattern. Islamic culture joined with the indigenous to form a syncretic mixture in all regions of Indonesia, but Javanese syncretism is distinctive. In the outer islands, the mix is typically between Islam and tribal custom; in Java, Islam is joined with a peasant animism and an elitist Hinduism. Such a mixed culture is known as *abangan* as well as by other (usually derogatory) terms. The *abangan* do not pray, fast, pay the tax, and they care nothing for making the pilgrimage to Mecca. They scandalize the purist *santri* by their unwieldy mixtures of the local and the Islamic,

as when they ascribe the origin of such items as magical
daggers to legendary mystical saints of Islam and hold communal ceremonies which unite all possible spirits with the
deities and heroes of Islam. Just as *santri* purity is symbolized by white, so *abangan* syncretism is symbolized by red;
"abang" is Javanese for "red." In recent years, the term has
acquired a new and for some, threatening, meaning since many
abangan became Communists—enemies of the Muslims owing to the
Marxist denial of God.

The syncretism of Islam and Javanism achieved its highest
civilization through the sultanate of Mataram, established in
central Java in the seventeenth century A.D., and existing on
a much reduced scale to the present day. Claiming no god-king
stature, the Sultan of Mataram was, nevertheless, "He who
holds the world in his lap." For some of his subjects, he
still shines with the divine light; traditionally, his mystical power was believed to waft through the corridors, streets,
and fields of his kingdom to instill an atmosphere of security.
Within this secure order, the lords established their own
medieval-style kingdoms, supported by a worshipful peasantry
and surrounded by an urban white collar aristocracy. The
lords and gentlemen of Mataram, like their aristocratic coun-
terparts in medieval Europe, combined the manly arts of the
military with refinement of manner and culture. The gentleman
should master the elaborate protocol of Javanese etiquette, he
should know dance, music, poetry, and mysticism, and he should
take part in the tournaments or jousts held at the provincial
palaces. Supported by a system of trade, transport, and communications which was only rudimentary, Mataram achieved an
impressive civilization which was in fundamentals more Hinduist than Muslim.

Westernization

Into this somewhat idyllic Asian island society thrust the
grasping hand of the West. The Dutch pulled ashore at Bantam,
Java, in 1596, and proceeded to join the Portuguese, the
English, and the Spanish in a quest for profit in the tropical waters. Ultimately they triumphed in the battle for dominance in Indonesia. Forming the East Indies Trading Company
(VOC), the Dutch systematically exploited disputes among
localized kingdoms in order to gain eventual control over
them. In the eighteenth century, the Dutch forces won a major
victory over Mataram. They then divided that kingdom into
two principalities, Jogjakarta and Surakarta, and established
puppet sultans in those two central Javanese courts. In time,
the remainder of Java as well came to be controlled by the

VOC, which ruled indirectly through the local lords and aristocrats who continued to extract produce from the peasants but
would now hand it over to the Dutch.

During the eighteenth and nineteenth centuries, the hierarchical structure of Mataram remained intact and was even
strengthened thanks to the military backing of the Dutch.
Rendered politically and militarily impotent, the Mataram
courts turned inward and concentrated on refining their culture. During the eighteenth and nineteenth centuries, the
courts were the center for the evolution of incredibly subtle
and refined dances, music, and drama. The courts also created
a new language: a stratified elaboration of the Javanese,
such that entirely separate vocabularies were employed in addressing each stratum of society. These hierarchical forms
soon filtered down to the villages, and the peasant would address the aristocrat after the model of the subject addressing
the king. Stratified Javanese language remains prominent in
the culture today.

Before 1870, the Dutch had penetrated only lightly into
islands outside Java, but now they opened the Indies to com-
merce and industry resulting in developers swarming to the
outer islands and a correlated spread of the colonial government. Colonialism was not always received peacefully, as
shown by the famous war between the Dutch and Atjehnese in
northern Sumatra; the militant Atjehnese Muslims held off the
Dutch forces for 25 years. But by the beginning of the twentieth century, plantation economy, coupled with a certain degree of industrialization and an expansion of colonial government, was established in Indonesia. These developments provided opportunity for two flourishing social types: the bureaucrat and the entrepreneur.

Among the Indonesian entrepreneurs, the Chinese were most
successful; they were the middlemen between the western busi-
nesses and the natives. The *santri,* too, were active in
smaller enterprises. On Java, they led in the manufacture of
batik cloth and *kretek* cigarettes. On Sumatra, they became
commercial growers of rubber trees. Although tradespeople
constituted a miniscule percentage of the total Indonesian
labor force, they were a large percentage of the *santri*
minority.

In the wake of the disruption of Indonesian life that derived from industrialization and commercialization, the
Netherlands replaced its so-called Liberal policy with the
so-called Ethical one: the colonial government endeavored to
provide new services in education and social welfare. New
services required new bureaucracy and new bureacracy new
bureaucrats. Many of these were recruited from among Indonesians of less than elite status, but these became a new
elite by virtue of their education and government posts, in

contrast to the old elite whose status derived from birth.
The Dutch Native Schools, enrolling some 20,000 students in
1915 and some 45,000 by the end of the colonial period in 1940,
provided the first mass opportunity for Indonesians to acquire
the Dutch language and Western education necessary for posts
in the colonial government. The prestige of an academic degree and a bureaucratic position became so great that, in many
areas, worship of the diploma and the white collar rivalled
that of the old sacred relics.

Movements

Westernization evoked in Indonesia as elsewhere feelings of
alienation and confusion. Most of the major Indonesian movements of twentieth century colonial Indonesia could be traced
to these problems as well as to economics and politics.
The earliest movements were cultural rather than political.
They divided along the purist/syncretist line. The most important syncretist movements were Budi Utomo (High Endeavor)
and Taman Siswa (Garden of Learning), both founded during the
early twentieth century by Javanese aristocrats. Budi Utomo
sought to revitalize the Hindu-Buddhist culture of old Java as
a way of rediscovering balance, refinement, and stability lost
through Westernization. Taman Siswa, which claimed inspiration
from India's Tagore and Ghandi, had similar objectives within
the field of education. Founding private schools to serve as
alternatives to the colonial ones, Taman Siswa aspired for an
education that was communal and family-like; teachers were to
feel as "brothers in learning."
The most important educational and cultural movement among
the *santri* was Muhammadijah, founded in 1912 in central Java.
Like the syncretic cultural movements, Muhammadijah endeavored
to respond to the pressures and alienation of change by rediscovering an older identity. It did so in a manner both aggressive and progressive. It was part of a wider movement in the
Malayo-Muslim world known as the Kaum Muda or "New Faction."
In the late nineteenth century, the advent of the steamship
encouraged Malayo-Indonesian Muslims to make the pilgrimage
to Mecca. In time, the Malayo-Indonesian community was the
largest of any foreign one in the holy city, and many who
travelled to Mecca remained to study in Cairo. By the early
twentieth century, several of the Malay, Indonesian, Arab,
and Indian citizens of the Malayo-Indonesian Muslim world had
come under the influence of the pioneer teacher of Islamic
modernism, Muhammad Abduh of Cairo's Azhar University. These
students returned to Singapore, at that time the center of the
Southeast Asian Muslim world. They founded schools, journals,
and organizations that spread the doctrine of Islamic modern-

ism into Malaya and the Indies, where they became known as the
Kaum Muda of Malayo-Indonesian Islam. They were known also as
a "reformasi" or "reformation" movement.

These reformists pressed for a return to the fundamental
truths of the Islamic text and tradition, the Qur'an and Hadith.
They rejected other authorities, including the venerated *kijai*
and the other Muslim teachers and scholars who taught the or-
nate philosophies and legal systems of medieval Islam. These
interpretations, the reformists argued, were not of divine origin, whereas the Qur'an was. Believers were exhorted to pursue the method of *idjtihad,* to analyze and dissect the original
Arabic scriptures in order to read for themselves the divine
message.

The holy scripture did not favor the syncretic practices.
Animism, Hinduism, and Sufism therefore must be ruthlessly
excised from the life of the true believer. The spread of
reformism accentuated the distinction between the syncretists,
those who practice the pre-Islamic religion, and the reformists, who ideally did not. The nonreformist *santri* stood between syncretists and reformists. Both were targets of the
reformist movement, which sought to purify the religious life
of the Muslim of all that is not Islam.

During the half-century since the florescence of reformism
in Southeast Asia, the movement has evolved differently in
the varied regions. Only in Indonesia does the Muslim reformation remain a major, organized force. Represented in the
early twentieth century by numerous small movements, the
reformation in Indonesia has coalesced into a few large regional movements and a single, powerful national one: Muhammadijah. Boasting hundreds of branches and millions of members distributed throughout the islands, Muhammadijah is certainly the most powerful Islamic movement ever to exist in
Southeast Asia. Essentially a missionary movement which
teaches pure Islam, Muhammadijah has made impressive social
and educational contributions as well. Its clinics, orphanages, poorhouses, and hospitals, together with several thousand schools, render it the most important private, non-Chris-
tian social, educational, and religious organization in Indonesia. Its women's branch, 'Aisjijah, is probably the most
dynamic Muslim women's movement in the world. In short, Muhammadijah is an organization of importance and power in the
world's fifth largest nation.

Despite its prominence, Muhammadijah has by no means won
the contest of movements in Indonesia. From the start it com-
peted not only with the syncretic cultural movements but with
syncretically-oriented political movements as well. The year
Muhammadijah was founded (1912), the Indische Partij (I.P.)
and the Sarekat Islam (S.I.) were founded. The I.P. was the
first nationalist party of Indonesia, but it appealed mainly

to the Dutch-educated intelligentsia, it never grew large, and
it was short-lived. The S.I. was at first a union of *santri*
batik merchants—a kind of economic counterpart to the Muhammadijah—but it grew into Indonesia's first nationalist mass
movement. S.I. was led by the charismatic Tjokroaminoto, the
Javanese aristocrat who replaced the batik-merchant founder
and was seen by the masses as a mythical messiah who would
liberate them from colonial oppression. By 1917, S.I. became
associated with the Indonesian Communist Party (known after
1920 as P.K.I.), and for a time an unsteady alliance was main-
tained between atheists and theists: P.K.I. riots in west
Java and west Sumatra in 1926 and 1927 signalled the debut of
Muslim Communists.

   At the time of these outbreaks, which resulted in the crush-
ing of P.K.I. and were followed by the decline of the S.I.,
a young engineering student known as Sukarno founded a study
club that became known in 1927 as the Indonesian National
Party or P.N.I. Drawing on the imagery of his beloved syncretist shadow plays, Sukarno for a time was a tenuous member
of the Muhammadijah as he endeavored to link *santri* and
abangan views. He succeeded in creating and popularizing national symbols—a language, a flag, and the name Indonesia.
He appealed especially to the intelligentsia whose loss of
social identity he eased with an ideology promising community
and kinship. In his vision, the new Indonesian nation would
be a family, a village, and it would give alienated natives a
cozy shelter for their traditional personality.

Occupation, Revolution and Independence

   When the second World War began, the Japanese occupied Indonesia. Dutch colonialism ended in 1942. The Japanese dif-
fered from the Dutch in their attitude toward the native movements. The movements fitted their dream of a united Asia, and
they gave the Indonesians intensive training in the arts of
organization, propaganda and war.

   After defeat by the Allies, Japan encouraged Indonesia's
independence from the Dutch. Sukarno broadcast the declaration on August 17, 1945, but the Netherlands did not give up
its colony lightly. For five years the Indonesian guerilla
army fought in the jungles and mountains against the Dutch
for independence. The experience was rich with symbols such
as "struggle," "spirit," "freedom," and, of course, "revolution." The dynamic vision of revolution appealed to the
youth, who were to become a major force in the new nation.

   When Indonesia finally gained its independence in 1949, it
was composed of the same conflicting factions existing since
the beginning of the century. A basic cleavage was along the

santri/abangan division. The *santri* bloc included the traditionalist party, Nahdatul Ulama, which had developed in reac-
tion to Muhammadijah, and the reformist Masjumi, which for a
time was affiliated with Muhammadijah. The *abangan*-oriented
group included the Communists (P.K.I.) and the Nationalists
(P.N.I.). The *santri* bloc appealed more strongly to the merchant class and the outer islands, the syncretist-nationalist-
Communist to the Javanese laboring class and the white collar
bureaucrat.

Bitter competition between these factions during the 1950s
encouraged President Sukarno to unpack his old idea of syncretic unity. This he presented under the name Guided Democracy. Guided Democracy was organized around the notion of
decision-making through consensus in an idealized peasant
village. Eschewing the mechanics of decision by vote, Sukarno
established a sprawling system of consensual bodies all under
his authoritarian, if undisciplined, control. Ideologically,
Guided Democracy evoked memories of Hinduist-syncretist the-
osophy for it formulated grand visions symbolized by such
acronyms as Manipol-Usdek, the letters of which represented
the "just and prosperous society," organized under "socialism
á la Indonesia," financed by Guided Economy, and fitted to the
traditional "Indonesian identity."

The downfall of the brilliantly charismatic Sukarno came in
the aftermath of Gestapu in 1965. Gestapu was a bloodbath in
which the army, supported in part by *santri,* slaughtered hundreds of thousands of supposed Communists. For a time, the
P.K,I., which had grown to several million members, became
dormant. Now *santri* looked for a revival, and reformist
santri prepared to reestablish the Masjumi party which Sukarno
had banned in 1960. Suharto, the new President, forced the
reformists to be content with a less powerful party, the Partai Muslimin Islam, or P.M.I., whose leader was Djarnawi,
author of the Preface to this work. In the election of 1971,
P.M.I. joined all the other parties in winning only a few
parliamentary seats. Indeed, the winner was the technocratic,
antipolitical central government organization Golkar, whose
motto was "Development before Ideology." It is worth remem-
bering, however, that the present study was carried out in
1970, prior to the 1971 election. While Muhammadijans already suspected what the outcome of the election would be,
they still enjoyed a feast of power compared to the famine of
the anti-*santri* years of Sukarno.

We turn now to the Muhammadijah, to trace its career through
the phases of modern Indonesian history to the present day.

CHAPTER THREE

Origins: *Biographical Analysis of the Founder of Muhammadijah*

Muhammadijah was founded in 1912 in the Central Javanese city of Jogjakarta by Kijai Hadji Achmad Dahlan. As with other movements, stories of the founder provide a source of inspiration. In speeches, conversations and other oral accounts, one hears anecdotes about this modest, diligent, driving reformer. Many of these, together with available historical facts (which seem, in the main, accurate), have been collected in the official Muhammadijah biography of Dahlan: *Riwajat Hidup K. H. A. Dahlan, Dan Perdjoangannja* (Life History of K. H. A. Dahlan, His Action and Struggle), which was written by H. M. Junus Anis, himself a former president of the organization and an influential leader. This work is supplemented by a popular version (identical in the main to the official one): *K. H. A. Dahlan, Reformer, Islam Indonesia* (K. H. A. Dahlan, Indonesian Muslim Reformer) by Solichin Salam.

These texts will be confronted historically, ethnographically, and psychologically. The first task is simply to summarize the biographer's narrative. The second is to take account of socio-cultural contexts within which this narrative must be interpreted. The third is to construct, insofar as the materials permit, the subjective processes by which Dahlan's life unfolds—something of Dahlan's psychology. Throughout, one must remember the nature of the form. A biography is not a life but a portrayal of a life, and due regard must be shown for the biographer's style and purpose. A first question is whether it is permissible to apply the term biography at all to a document coming from a civilization whose narratives from the ancient Javanese myths of creation

to modern Javanese fiction embody exotic conceptions of time
and history. Fortunately, at the surface level, our task appears simple. The works are, in outline at least, straight-
forwardly chronological in a conventional, Western-like format. Junus Anis divides his book into five phases: "Time of
Infancy and Childhood," "Education," "As Husband and Father,"
"Struggle," and "The End of His Life." This sequence will be
followed in analyzing the biographical account.

Infancy and Childhood

"Jogjakarta is known inside and outside the nation as a city
of struggle," writes Junus Anis, "though from its location
one would assume that it is a region of peace." Anis goes on
to observe that this court city of the empire of Mataram,
nestled in the agrarian rice bowl of Central Java and revered
for its aristocratic Hinduist and *abangan* civilization, is
"distant from the crowds and noise of the outside world."
Yet Jogjakarta was the natal home of the first nationalist
Indonesian revolutionary, Diponegoro, and it was the revolutionary capital of the new Indonesian republic. "Thus it is
proper that Jogjakarta be termed a *City of Revolution*."
    In Jogjakarta, writes Junus, is found the "Kampung Kauman...
situated near the palace of the Sultan, famed as a residence
of the pious." Writing not long after Dahlan's death, the
eminent Islamologist Pijper (1934, p. 1) elaborates Junus'
image of the Kauman at that time. Pijper describes this
crowded but affluent ghetto or casbah-like quarter as the
place of residence of pious fabric manufacturers and mosque
officials. Owing to an old privilege granted by the sultan,
only *santri* live here: Chinese and Christians are excluded.
Indeed, so is the world, in the form of such *abangan* pleas-
ures as Javanese percussion orchestra music and dancing girls,
and at the time of the Islamic fast month no one would dare
eat, drink, or smoke during the day in the Kauman. In the
evenings, the sound of Qur'anic chanting issues from houses
while on the streets men and women scurry to places of prayer.
This pious, commercial quarter was to be the lifelong residence of K. H. A. Dahlan and the birthplace of Muhammadijah.
    In this Kauman, "in the nineteenth century there lived a
religious teacher named Kijahi Hadji Abubakar bin Kijahi H.
Sulaiman." ("Bin" means "son of," reflecting a patrilineal
emphasis among the *santri* which is lacking in the bilateral
kinship of the *abangan*; Junus here sets the stage for the
birth of the son by citing the pedigree of the father.)
Hadji Abubakar, the father, held the office of *chatib* (the
religious official responsible for the Friday sermon) in the
Great Mosque of the Sultanate of Jogjakarta.

Plate 1: An Alley of the Kauman, Jogjakarta.

"In the year 1868 (Christian calendar) or 1285 H. (Muslim calendar), the family of H. Abubakar was blessed by God with the birth of the fourth son. He was named Mohammad Darwisj." The biographer apologizes that only the year of birth, not the day is known, and here he throws in relief Darwisj's deviation from the traditional *abangan* who remembers the day

but not the year. The *abangan* calendar is cyclical and punc-
tuate, emphasizing not the progressive passage of time but
periodic meshing of such simultaneous cycles as seven- and
five-day weeks. Since the days of meshing are auspicious they
are celebrated, remembered, and they serve as the reference
point for such occasions as birth. The *santri* calendar is
more linear, as is reflected in this portion of the biography,
which is concerned with the passing of unrepeatable years—in
a word, history—rather than the repetition of days.

Both the patrilineal and the historical are revealed in the
biographer's genealogy that traces Darwisj's ancestry for 11
generations on his father's side, but only four generations
on his mother's. The pattern rather resembles that of some
santri in the Jogjakarta area, who trace their membership in
patrilineal clans. Anis mentions Darwisj's mother, but only
to say that her father, like the father of Darwisj, was an
official of the Great Mosque: "From this we know that the
child named Mohammad Darwisj was born into a pious family
and lived in a religious atmosphere."

A certain lack of interest in memory of childhood (which
may be typical of Muhammadijans in general to judge from
their accounts of their own life histories) is reflected in
this biography of Darwisj's childhood. We are told only that
he was "diligent, honest, and helpful," and that he was "ex-
ceptionally clever and industrious with his hands, with which
he constructed playthings that made him popular among his
playmates." Remembered experience, then, is replaced by
moralizing and attending to the practical.

Mention of the use of hands and the construction of toys is
unique among Javanese biographies or autobiographies and
suggests a value which is atypically Javanese. While crafts,
such as the construction of puppets and daggers, are certainly
part of the syncretist Javanese tradition, there is not the
emphasis on construction toys such as building blocks that
one finds in the technological societies. Instead, one sees
dolls for girls and hobby horses for boys, a situation which
one Javanese youth interpreted in an interesting if forced
analogy: "Instead of building things, we like to ride toy
horses—thus learning how to mount to higher status." Possibly
Dahlan's alleged interest in making things and Junus' mention
of it reflects the concentration of small craftsmen-merchants
within the Kauman.[1] In any case, Dahlan's manual dexterity

---

[1] Max Weber (1964) suggests that just this type of occupation
breeds a propensity toward salvation religions like Christianity and Islam. Weber argues that artisans differ from
peasants because they do crafts rather than farm, and thus
control their production rather than being subject to the

as a child foreshadows Junus' characterization of him as a
man not of words, but of work.

Education

The maturation of a pious Muslim boy follows a common pattern throughout Southeast Asia: a centrifugal movement from
the female to the male, the domestic to the public, the play-
ful to the Islamic. The *santri* boy moves from the cozy, fe-
male-dominated household (the so-called matrifocal household
in Java) out to the male-dominated school and mosque, and finally on the pilgrimage to distant Mecca.

What few facts are provided suggest that Dahlan followed
this typical pattern; he began to learn the elements of Islamic doctrine and chanting from his parents and in a neighborhood school. He was circumcised probably before age ten
and then he began to join his male kinsmen in praying at the
mosque. By puberty, he may have become a student at one of
the austere and remote Islamic schools, the *pesantren* which
typically cement attitudes of independence, male solidarity,
and commitment to the Islamic cause. Certainly such schooling forces a break from the local community, such as the
hierarchical, Hinduist court-complex of Jogjakarta.

Dahlan's next move was the pilgrimage to Mecca, which he
was requested to make by his father. Darwisj's biographer
reports that when he was "rather large" he was "ordered" to
go; his expenses were paid by a businesswoman aunt. Of
Darwisj's stay in Mecca, it is stated only that he lived in
the "sacred land several years in order to pursue religious
studies such as Qur'anic exegesis, theology, religious law,
and astronomy."

Eventually the pilgrim came home, influenced by the writings of the Egyptian reformist Abduh, to judge from works
found in Dahlan's library. As was customary for the returned
pilgrim, Dahlan's name was changed, from Darwisj to Ahmad
Dahlan.

---

whims of nature. And their products result in payment directly from customers. Such a way of life, Weber suggests,
is compatible with a salvation religion which postulates
that humans exercise some degree of control over their behavior and that the character of this behavior determines
whether one is rewarded or punished by God.

Husband and Father

Junus Anis begins his description of the postpilgrimage phase of K. H. A. Dahlan's life by stating:

> ...K. H. Ahmad Dahlan for his entire life was *chatib* (official)...of the Sultan Mosque of Jogjakarta, replacing his father. It is no secret that the Sultan Mosque of Jogja has 12 *chatibs* .... As a *chatib,* he received a monthly salary of 7 guilders. In addition, the honored-he [*Jang Terhormat*—an Indonesian term of respect] manufactured and sold batik fabric. His trade took him to East Java, West Java, and nearby lands ....

From observation of the Kauman today, one can imagine Dahlan's life alternating between a cozy and pious routine in these cramped quarters and strenuous travel, by outrigger boat, coal-burning train, horse-drawn wagon, and on foot among the noisy and competitive marketplaces of the town, and ports. Though Dahlan would deliver occasional sermons in the Great Mosque in the shadow of the Sultan's palace, and he doubtless enjoyed evening study-sessions and dawn-prayers followed by the sipping of coffee with his fellow worshippers in the Kauman, much of his time must have been spent on the road. This peripatetic pattern remains a core of *santri* life and of Muhammadijah.

"K. H. Ahmad Dahlan married Siti Walidah (later famed as Njai Dahlan), daughter of Kijahi Penghulu Hadji Fadhil." Siti's religious teacher father was Dahlan's mother's brother. Later he was to marry four additional wives, divorcing each after a short while but retaining "Mother Walidah" until his death. Such serial/simultaneous polygamy was typical of Muslim leaders of his day.

Struggle

"Struggle" *(perdjuangan)* is a standard category in modern Indonesian narration of life history. It usually follows a perfunctory account of childhood, youth, and marriage, and this struggle is usually in a collective context, a movement. Finally it is against something—some force or condition. It is the struggle that is one's calling, that gives one's life meaning, that culminates in retirement and death.

This formula is closely followed in the biography of Dahlan which titles a section *Perdjuangan*, subsumes it under the Muhammadijah movement, and sets it against certain forces and conditions. These latter are schematically listed by Anis as Mysticism, Hindu-Buddhism, Feudalism, and Colonialism. Each is felt to have led to the decline of Islam. Syncretic mysticism fostered preoccupation with the "inner life and the after life" at the expense of social problems; Hindu-Buddhism contaminated the purity of Islam; Feudalism deified royalty in place of Allah; and Colonialism encouraged Christianity.

Dahlan's struggle against these things is portrayed as dedicated, but not fiery or revolutionary; no wrathful wielder of the sword, he waged a struggle that was calm, systematic, and less a protest than reform.

Only a single instance of Dahlan's direct protest against the established order (here "Feudalism, Syncretism, and Colonialism" all united as the Jogja court) is described in Junus' biography and this Junus omits from the section entitled "His Struggle." Indeed, as though to signal its deviancy from the overall thrust of Dahlan's effort, the event is relegated to a catchall section entitled "Several Anecdotes." The incident occurred soon after Dahlan's return from his first pilgrimage. Trained in astronomy, Dahlan demonstrated the erroneous compass orientation of the Great Mosque by chalking in the correct one. This act incurred the wrath of the chief priest of the palace, who burnt down Dahlan's prayer house one evening during the fast month. Struck down, Dahlan prepared to leave Jogja but he was intercepted at the railway station by his older brother who convinced him to stay.

A second incident, also reported among the "Several Anecdotes," suggests that in manner Dahlan kept a polite and humble attitude toward the Jogjakarta court. He wished to bring before the ruler, the Paduka Sri Sultan, a suggestion concerning the holding of the Garabeg feast. So that Dahlan could "speak freely and convey the contents of his heart without being dazzled by the Paduka Sri Sultan and the nobles of his staff," this personage received Dahlan in a darkened room at midnight. Although the biographer considers that the incident reflects Dahlan's bravery in daring to speak to exalted royalty, the Western reader is perhaps more struck by the submissiveness and politeness; Dahlan is here no Luther shouting "Here I stand" to the princes.

To appreciate Dahlan's position, the near-divine status of the sultan of Jogjakarta must be understood. The Sultan was successor to Mohammad, Apostle of Allah, and king of one of the three remaining courts of the great empire of Mataram. The Sultan's birthday must be celebrated every five weeks, and through such ceremonies as the Islamic-Hinduist Garabegs he was believed to sustain the socio-cosmic order; were the rites neglected "the heavenly guardians of the mountains and the state *pusakas* (magical relics) might feel offended and evil would befall the State and its People" (Selosoemardjan 1962, p. 28). Dahlan was merely an employee of the court, one of the Islamic officials whose duties included performing the Garabegs.

Under the circumstances, it is also remarkable that Dahlan was permitted to remain an official in the Sultan's Mosque. Dutch reports of the day portray more forcefully than Junus Anis his differences with the authorities. It is the Dutch observer Rinkes, not Anis, who reports that Dahlan's chalking of the proper orientation of the Great Mosque resulted in his being exiled for a time (Mailrapport 1913), and he describes Dahlan's small Arabic school as "in the middle of the arch-conservative palace complex, an abomination to the native authorities (Mailrapport 1914)." Yet Rinkes' report, written two years after the founding of Muhammadijah, states that Dahlan is still a mosque official, and he apparently remained so until his death.

The other establishment against which Dahlan could have revolted is the colonial government, and Solichin Salam depicts Muhammadijah in this light:

> ...the birth of Muhammadijah was a response to the challenge thrown down to the Indonesian people in general and Indonesian Muslims in particular. ...Its birth was to free the Muslim community and Indonesian peoples from the snares of colonialism, conservatism, dogmatism, formalism, traditionalism, and isolationism. (Salam 1965 p. 54)

But no specific anticolonialist protest by Dahlan is mentioned, and classified Dutch reports written during the time of Dahlan suggest that he was highly regarded by the colonial regime. Indeed, the Dutch official, Rinkes, idolized Dahlan in 1913, as a kind of Indonesian epitome of the Calvinist ethic, an

> energetic, militant, intelligent man some 40 years of age, obviously with some Arab blood and strictly orthodox but with a trace of tolerance. ...Personally H. Dahlan makes a good impression: one notes a man of character and a will to *do*, which is not seen *everyday* in either the Indies or Europe. (Mailrapport, 1914)

In contrast, Hadji Samanoedi, founder of the anticolonialist mass movement, Sarekat Islam, is to Rinkes a dissolute boor:

> Of about 35 years of age, with sensuous not unattractive face that shows his years. Rumor has it that earlier he gambled and ran with loose women, or changed wives in the meantime, while his fortunes derived from producing batik and lending money to the *Prijaji* [aristocrats] of Solo.... That this man, who is wholly uncultivated, also poorly educated in Islam, and apparently possesses merely the good merchant's savvy, should have purpose and expecta-

tion that his association should expand is difficult to
understand.... (Mailrapport 1914).

Nine years later, after the Muhammadijah was in full motion,
the Dutch opinion of Dahlan remained favorable, according to
the well-known sociologist and official, Schrieke (Mailrapport
1922); and even the Catholic missionary, Bakker, one of Muhammadijah's most adamant opponents, wrote that Dahlan himself
was a man of tolerance toward Christians (F. L. O. Bakker 1925).
    Concerning the movement itself, the Dutch reports consistent-
ly regard it as rational and safe; thus, a Mailrapport notes
approvingly that Dahlan has "avoided the tactics of independence movements, late night, secret meetings with *Dzikir*
[trance-inducing chants] and the like" (Mailrapport 1914)
which were associated with uprisings elsewhere in the colony,
and Schrieke (Mailrapport 1922) advised the government not to
oppose the organization so long as it sticks to its original
missionary and educational objectives.
    Dahlan's struggle, then, was not a violent and revolutionary
protest. What was it, and how did it start?
    Junus Anis depicts Dahlan's movement as beginning when he
travelled about trading. Wherever he went, he encouraged religious teachers to cooperate in "spreading Islam and improving
the Muslim community" through such activities as study conferences and Qur'anic chanting contests. During these early
years, Dahlan also participated in the syncretist-Javanist
organization, Budi Utomo, in Jogjakarta, and he associated
with theosophists, mystics, and even Christians: "All of this
was used as a means to bring about an orientation for the
development of a Muslim missionary organization."
    Dahlan's early nucleus was his own students, which is typi-
cal of Indonesian Muslim reformism—it usually centers around
schools. Twelve individuals, including students and fellow
teachers from the various schools at which Dahlan was teaching, reportedly urged Dahlan to organize a reformist organization. Dahlan agreed, and when they asked him the organization's name, he replied, "Muhammadijah." On November 18, 1912,
when Dahlan was approximately 44 years old, he founded the
Muhammadijah in Jogjakarta.
    Dahlan was "ordered" to go to Mecca, and he was "urged" to
found Muhammadijah, reports Junus. Here the prophetic theme
of being called is indistinguishable from a Javanese modesty
and other-directedness reflected in a biographical account
which accords to the other, instead of the self, the role of
initiating action. In any case, once the founding was accomplished, the role of Dahlan is portrayed as a highly goal-
oriented and systematic one. At this point, however, the
narrative ceases to portray the individual life and it begins

to portray the collective movement; it is now the organization's goals and plans that are enunciated.

Summarizing the thrust of the struggle after 1912, Junus Anis outlines the Muhammadijah goals (essentially to restore pure Islam), its committees (missionary, youth, etc.), and its periods (depending on who was head), the number of its branches, schools, clinics, and hospitals, and congresses. He summarizes the endeavors (*amal usaha*) of Dahlan and Muhammadijah under three headings: religious, social, and educational.

While much of this activity is bureaucratic and reveals little about Dahlan except his organizational skill and diligence, of special interest are the remarks by Salam about Dahlan's view of the role of women; this view mixes the rationalizing implications of reformist psychology and the traditionalism of the Islamic conception of sexuality.

Dahlan organized a school to teach women Islam, he encouraged them to speak in public, and to organize. In short, he strove to include women as effectively functional instruments within reformism. Yet while encouraging the organizational emancipation of women, Dahlan also intensified the sexual segregation of men from women. Thus, his stated reason for encouraging women doctors was so women need not reveal their private parts to male doctors. He got Kauman women to give up the jewelry and dresses that advertised their feminine charms, and he taught them to cover the head with a scarf.

Dahlan's efforts were not greeted everywhere by applause. He was called infidel, even Christian, by conservative *santri*, and he was reportedly threatened with murder at least once. His biographers stress that in the face of all obstacles, he was a model of calm determination: this image is expressed also in remembrances of Dahlan that are the legends of the movement today.

The End of His Life

When Dahlan became ill in his fifties, he was advised to seek a change of climate at a retreat near Mount Bromo. "But even there he continued to work (doing missionary organization and preaching), until he got worse instead of better;" his industriousness is suggested by 17 out-of-town trips for Muhammadijah which Dahlan made during the year before he died. When his wife begged him to rest, he replied:

I must work hard, in order to lay the first stone in this great movement. If I am late or cease, due to my illness, there is no one who will build the groundwork. I already feel that my time is almost gone, thus if I

. work as fast as possible, what remains can be brought
to perfection by another.

"What he said was apparently true, for not long after he could
not rise from his bed," writes Junus. When Dahlan's death was
near, he summoned friends and his brother-in-law to delegate
tasks to his successors. He died February 23, 1923, at his
home, Kauman 59, Jogjakarta.

Comment: Reformist Character

The biography of Dahlan concludes with the biographer's assessment of the character *(kepribadian)* of Dahlan. Solichin
Salam (1963) writes:

> His type of personality was *sepi ing pamrih* [Javanese for
> "tranquil in lacking self-interest"] yet *rame ing gawe*
> [*active in work*]. He was a man who was *ichlas* [stoic,
> devoted, steadfast]...Kiai Dahlan had the spirit of the
> *satria* [the Hindu-Javanese conception of the warrior who,
> like Ardjuna in the *Bhagavagita,* carries out the code
> of his station, waging the outer struggle while at peace
> inside].

Precisely the same terms—*sepi ing pamrih, rame ing gawe,
ichlas,* and *satria*—are applied to Dahlan by Junus Anis. These
terms are central also in the teachings of Javanese mystical
philosophies and in Javanese values in general. In the end,
Anis sums up his fellow Jogjarkartan by a set of virtues more
Javanese than Islamic.

An associated Javanese value is the hierarchical one, *hormat,*
reverence for statuses higher than one's own and for hierarchy
as such. Though a reformist, Dahlan had *hormat,* whether in
his custom of speaking the stratified Javanese language, in
his courtesy to the Sultan and the Dutch government, or in his
inner humility. No protestor in the ill-mannered sense,
throughout his career he remained the faithful servant of the
hierarchy. Within his status, he happened to lead a pragmatic
and positive movement to purify the faith, but the movement
never exploded the status, which explains how he, a reformist,
could remain an official of the court mosque, deeply conservative, until he died.

Least Javanese and most Islamic about Dahlan was his stress
on hellfire and damnation. Anis' first quotation from Dahlan's
Teachings and Pearls of Wisdom is, "We humans are given as a
trust only one life in this world. After you die, will you be
saved or be damned?" Other quotations carry the same message,
which recall the driving force of the Christian Calvinists.
Yet this salvation theology is not a leitmotif in the

biography; indeed, it is not mentioned except in this final, isolated section on the *Pearls*. Quietly, Dahlan's concern with salvation must have motivated his struggle, but what is depicted is the steady dedication of a man determined to carry through the precepts of a reformist mandate expressed in his organization and its creed.

Methodical, orderly, struggling continuously for cultural purification, Dahlan mistrusted sensuality and the giving way to forces of instinct, which is the notorious *hawa nafsu* of Malayo-Muslim psychological theory. Note his drive to stifle the sensuality of women. While vulgar psychology might reduce this motive to some unconscious fear, such as of the woman-power of his many wives, any such emotion is subordinate to the broader logic of reformism; the reformist struggles to purify the world of magic, mystery, and sensuality in the name of law, scripture, and the supreme God, to control the *hawa nafsu* through *achlaq* (ethics) and *akal* (rationality).

Returning to the question of Dahlan's treatment of women, it must be emphasized that while he restrained their public sensuality, he increased their organizational power. The same is true of feminist movements; they strive to replace women's sexual valence with political force. It is remarkable that Dahlan was able to emphasize the rationalizing stream of Islam to liberate women to the extent that he did, while de-emphasizing that part of Islam which supports patriliny, polygyny, and a legal system rendering women second-class citizens.

Absent from the biography of Dahlan is the intense inner struggle known in Christian autobiographical and biographical accounts which depict a person obsessed by the need to achieve justification by purging himself of guilt and sin. The surface results of Dahlan's reformation were not unlike those of a Luther, a Calvin, or a Zwingli: the stripping of ritual to its essentials, delivery of sermons in the vernacular, reliance on the book instead of the priest. But the formulation of Luther, meaningful only within a culture imbued with the concept of original sin, was also an inner solution to a torment peculiar to himself. Less subjective in content, the reformation of Dahlan was a legalistic attempt to impose a Middle Eastern ethic on a Malayo-Indonesian society.

Like many reformists and revolutionaries, Dahlan began his struggle only after an experience of isolation—a "moratorium," in *pesantren* and pilgrimage. During these years of quest and study, Dahlan must have undergone the profound psychological experience of transferring emotion from parents and kin to teachers and teachings; recall the tradition of the *pesantren* student developing a mystical bond to his teachers. But this experience remained within a traditional social framework.

Dahlan took the pilgrimage at the command of his father and
with the fullest sanction of his *santri* culture and community;
he was doing what every good Muslim boy should do.

His return, too, was securely within the local social system. He took his father's place, in familial, occupational,
and Islamic spheres, and by his thirties he had a large family, prominent position, and many students. In contrast to
the Christian biographical tradition of celibacy and isolation while changing the world (think of Christ and Paul),
Dahlan could follow Muhammad's example of polygyny and community in the midst of reform.

The concept of biography is itself alien to the syncretist
culture; biography was introduced by Islam. Syncretist writings today include the biographical, especially when dealing
with the heroes of the revolution (who exemplify the syncretist's own paths of rationalization), but biographies are
still most in evidence among the reformist *santri*; the Muhammadijah appears to be the only Indonesian movement that publishes a biographical series, of which the work on Dahlan is
an example. Despite the biographical emphasis, however, the
reformist biographical form is not identical to that familiar
to the West. The linear, chronological format of the biographies of Dahlan is divided in the familiar phases of childhood, education, and the struggle. But little attention is
given to the development of personality through these experiences. Especially in what we are accustomed to term the
formative years, the treatment is so sketchy and episodic as
to give the impression that the biographer desires simply to
report a few events to express a conventionalized category of
time rather than to work through a process of personal formation. Here at the level of individual history is an equivalent to the epochal pattern in the Malayo-Indonesian conception of national history—a concern with characterizing stereo-
typed but richly symbolic epochal categories of chronology
while ignoring the dynamics which lead from one epoch to the
next.

This apparent lack of cohesion expresses another level of
meaning. The scattered episodes of personal experience are
replaced by the integrated frame of reformist Islamic
ideology. Through the systematization of doctrine, ritual,
preaching, teaching, and, above all, the struggle, life becomes meaningful and focused. Critical in this synthesis is
the word. Like young Muhammadijans today who discuss their
evangelistic campaigns with the same fervor as Western ath-
letes talk about their sports, Dahlan integrated his life
around evangelism—the communication of the word. He was so
devoted to it that he preached himself to death. The life
of the word reflects a critical emphasis of Islam, which is
scripturalistic and legalistic; Islam, brought to its logical

perfection in reformism, is based on the Qur'anic law by contrast to Christianity which is more quintessentially biographical in that its root-metaphor is not the law at all, but the
life sacralized in the biography of Christ.

Noteworthy is the local and familial focus of these reformists. Unlike the Western-educated, secular Indonesia intelligentsia who, as Taufik Abdullah (1971, p. 16) has noted,
were frequently "absorbed into the *rantau* (expatriate) society permanently," the Islamic reformists came home. Each
entered his movement in the very community of birth; Dahlan
stayed in the Jogjakarta Kauman. And, as Alfian (1970) has
noted, they rooted their struggles in nexus of blood and
ethnicity; many of the earliest targets, members, and leaders
of the movement were Dahlan's own kinfolk. Though drawing on
pan-Islamic, pan-modern philosophies, the early reforms were
directed against those customs and beliefs which were the core
of localized and familial existence.

In sum, the founder as biographed embodies a psychology
that follows from the logic of reformism. His ancestry is
patrilineal, abstracted from the richer context of bilineal
kinship recognized by tradition. His life, too, is lineal,
shaving away irrelevancy and organized methodically toward
the goals of reform and salvation. This struggle takes prece-
dence over the intimacy and nostalgia of childhood, the
sensuality of women, and the ecstasy of mysticism, all of
which distract from the straight and narrow.

Despite his strong drive toward reform, Dahlan does not
make the radical break with the social order which, in many
movements, is associated with painful inner search and even-
tuates in ecstatic visions of a new order and an inspired
zeal to bring it to pass. Dahlan gives no evidence of having
experienced such ecstatic visions, and this lack may reflect
the extent to which he remained within the social order.
Though his pilgrimage required him to quit his home, he did
so in the company of friends, under the sanction of his community, and with the guidance of esteemed teachers. When he
returned home, he replaced his father as an official at the
Sultan's mosque and he settled into a cozy net of fellow
believers. Courageous and unrelenting in his struggle, he
carried it out within the confines of an intimate circle and
established structure.

CHAPTER FOUR

Development: Muhammadijah as an Organization 1923-1970

By the time of the death of K. H. A. Dahlan in 1923, the
Muhammadijah movement had become highly organized, though it
was still small. As is typical in movements and as Weber
would have expected, the organization was becoming bureaucratized: the varied activities of the founding leader differentiated into numerous functional units, and the mother-
organization differentiated into dispersed branches. These
developments, together with daily concerns of the Muhammadijah organization, are described in an annual report written
in 1923, the year of Dahlan's passing.

Opening by stating the movement's objective "to improve
and strengthen the work of Allah and man's fate in the after-
life," (Moehammadijah 1923, p. 6) the report proceeds to
describe features of organization. Muhammadijah in 1923
contains 2622 men and 724 women, most of whom reside in
Jogjakarta; it is headed by K. H. Ibrahim, and it is divided
into a number of committees.

The report then describes the past year's activities, which
included no less than 32 meetings, several of which resolved
in recommendations for actions, including support for the
election of a Caliph by the world movement of Muslims; a
resolution that someone write a history of the period of
K. H. A. Dahlan; requests to the government to permit Muslims
more control over their affairs; a protest against gambling
on the Jogjakarta public green; and a proposal that only
female physicians be permitted to treat female patients or
handle female corpses.

45

The report next describes the activities of the various
committees: *works*, including the building of mosques and
holding of Qur'anic readings; *education*, including the building of schools; *library*, the printing and preserving of books;
social welfare (which includes detailed description of the
schedule for bathing, feeding, eating, praying, and instructing in poorhouse and orphanage a minute-by-minute schedule
essentially the same as that reported to me by Jogjakarta
orphanages fifty years later); *tabligh*, the celebration of
special holidays, including the fast month, the prophet's
birthday (*Maulud*), and the prophet's ascent into heaven
(*Mi'radj*); and finally *budget*, which mentions 69,356 guilders
received and 66,076 spent, 6461 of this from government subsidy, the rest from the religious tax, school fees, subsidy
from the sultanate, and private donations. Of special interest is the report concerning the women's division, 'Aisjijah,
which states:

All female religious needs can be achieved and managed
by women themselves. ...for example, teaching religion
to other women, educating children, writing compositions
of use to women, washing the corpses of women, and all
else that strengthens the condition of mankind and can
be accomplished by women.... But that which is too much
for the capacity of women is the obligation of men.
This is in accord with the teachings of Islam: men
must support women (Moehammadijah 1923, p. 33).

The report also mentions schools for women leaders, women's
mosques and women's meeting-houses. Reflecting an apparent
obsession with schedules and plans, the report records that
each Friday some 20 women meet to write down all that they
have done each day. Each then asks Allah forgiveness for any
wrong-doings, and they calculate what proportion of time
these sins have consumed; the report states, "These record-
ings have the utility that one can know oneself how much that
is good has been done and, on the other hand, *how much time*
has been used doing things against Islam (Moehammadijah 1923,
p. 23, italics added). This group, known as 'Wal 'Asjri, was
led by R. H. Hadjid, a male leader.
    The report concludes by outlining the division of the Mu-
hammadijah into geographical branches—a development which
at this point had barely begun, since most of the membership
was still to be found in Jogjakarta.
    Numerous culturally interesting facts can be gleaned from
the report. It is in the Malay language, which signals a
Malayo-Muslim rather than Javanese or Dutch orientation, at
a time when these elitist languages carry prestige and importance in the Jogjakarta hierarchy. Salvation in the next

life is clearly stated as a primary goal, which reinforces
the "pearls" of Dahlan. The activism of women is impressive
(and this point will be elaborated later), but the 'Aisjijah
report subordinates and limits the role of women: "that
which is *too much* for the capacity of women is the obligation
of men." At the same time, the women use this point to ask
for the cooperation of the men, and they show a remarkable
Protestant-like systematization of life and self, in their
meticulous schedules for orphanages and in recording of time
spent daily on their sins.

In 1925, the Muhammadijah held an important congress in
Jogjakarta, and we are fortunate in having available excellent
first-hand observations of this affair. A classified report
to the Governor General of the Indies written by the well-
known Orientalist, R. Kern, described the public events of
the Congress with an attention to culturally-relevant facts
that equals standards of modern ethnography (Mailrapport 1925b).

Kern begins by locating the site of the six-day congress:
the veranda of a member of the nobility, Raden Wadana Djajang-
prokosa. Here, on a Saturday evening, is held the first
public congress meeting. Kern notes that a section of seats
was marked for each major social faction, such as students or
women. As was the custom of Muhammadijah in prewar times,
the women were seated behind a screen that divides the front
section from the middle.

Kern observes that the Muhammadijans differ from the courtly, syncretic Javanese aristocrats, in that they hold no
reception before the meeting. They announced its beginning
at 8:30 and it actually began at 9 (astonishingly punctual
for a Javanese public meeting). At the gathering were few
aristocrats, but primarily people of the merchant class.
Because some persons were of Sundanese and Madurese as well
as Javanese ethnicity, Malay as well as Javanese was spoken.
No Arabs were present. The ostensible leader of the gathering
was Kijai Hadji Ibrahim, *chatib* of the Great Mosque, although
Kern considers the real leader to be Hadji Fahroedin. Kern
observes that Fahroedin is clad in street clothes of Western
style, though with a Javanese headdress, and that many of the
younger men wear the Malay cap instead of the Javanese headdress. What Kern is pointing to by his observations on etiquette, language, ethnicity, occupation, punctuality and dress
is the lack of Javaneseness at the congress: syncretic Javanese culture is here replaced by a Malayo-Indonesian *santri*
culture.

After a schoolchildren's song, a child greets the assembly
in Arabic, is answered in turn, and all recite the opening
section of the Qur'an; Kern notes that these patterns (which
persist today) establish a bond between speaker and audience.
Fahroedin opens the program, and a certain Hadji Mochti

chants from the Qur'an after which these passages are transla-
ted into common Javanese so that the local and the unschooled
can understand; such translation, Kern notes, is a modern
trait designed to assure the communication of meaning as well
as of form.

Now follow reports, first a recital of woes by the secretary
of the organization who describes the obstacles it is encoun-
tering from Christians, government, and even the Sultan;
second, a more positive description by the head of the social
welfare and health committee (P.K.U.) of the good deeds it is
accomplishing, including free circumcision for any male.

The women then came forward, Kern says, one by one from behind the screen. They speak guardedly, in high Javanese and
Arabic rather than Malay. Kern says they give the impression
of reading remarks prepared by the men, and their message is
that women's place is in the home.

After additional reports by a "pathfinder" on the way scout-
ing develops the body to better serve Islam, and by a physician concerning the medical duties of the committee on health
and social welfare, it is midnight. Kern now observes a parallel between the course of the Muhammadijah meeting and the
performance of the ubiquitous syncretic Javanese shadow play.
In the shadow play, by midnight the various forces of action
are revealed and there appears a figure who encompasses all
of them and is at the same time comical. This is Semar, the
clown. Both a servant and a god, male and female, animal
and spiritual, this infinitely wise clown explains all reali-
ty by a syncretic philosophy of which he himself is a seminal
Javanese symbol. Kern now perceives a Muslim version of
Semar, a "genuinely Javanese figure" who is a clown and a syncretic philosopher and who appears at midnight when the conflicting forces of the meeting have come to a head.

This individual, Imam Bisri from Solo, need merely mount
the podium in his sloppy clothes and handle his glass of
lemonade to evoke laughter. And like Semar, he expresses a
syncretic philosophy, interpreting the Qur'an from the stand-
point of Javanese cosmology in order to reveal how it is a
source of "classification, unity, and opposition."

Listening to his words, his beautiful language—itself
a necessity for the Javanese—his listeners can let their
thoughts flow out, as it were, until they fill the entire universe, and then they are assured that Islam is
the wellspring of all.

Iman Bisri draws enthusiastic applause, and the meeting closes
at 1:30 A.M. with the sounding of the opening chapter of the
Qu'ran.

Kern does not describe the private sessions of the congress,

which he probably did not attend, but the final public meeting
which took place on the fifth day. Again, there are lectures.
One is by the young Junus Anis (later to become a leader in
the organization and author of the biography of K. H. A. Dahlan) on the history of Islam; a second by the leader of Ahma-
diyya, the radical Pakistani reformist Muslim organization
with which Muhammadijah was at that time cooperating; a third,
on the world history of marriage; and a fourth by R. Hadji
Hadjid, on Christianity. Hadjid then presents a play, which
is the final presentation described in Kern's report and apparently concludes the Congress. The play concerns a wealthy
santri in the traditionalist east Javanese region of Ponerogo
who sends his son to a *pesantren* only to discover that conditions in that traditionalist school have degenerated. What to
do? His faithful servant supplies the answer: send the son
to the Muhammadijah school (Muallimien) in Jogjakarta, where he
can get a varied education—facets of which are now demonstrated to the audience.
    To me, an observer of recent Muhammadijah meetings, this
perceptive report of a meeting in 1925 is exciting in its
suggestion of both constancy and change, and of underlying
cultural themes. Just as in practical and spiritual works
and in a concern with management of time, so is systematization and rationalization apparent in the behavior at the
Congress. The tradition of so-called elastic time is still
strong in contemporary Java, where meetings often start hours
after an announced time. Yet Kern reports a remarkable punctuality in the starting time of the Congress; this distinctively reformist trait, reminiscent of the compulsiveness of the
so-called Protestant Ethic in the West, is still notable in
Muhammadijah meetings today. Also noteworthy is the lack of
the reception, which seems to reflect a diminishing of the
ceremoniousness so central to Javanese, especially Jogjakartan, civilization. What appears to be happening is that the
aristocratic, Hinduist traditions of syncretic Javanese civilization are being purged within reformist circles; in their
place, to a degree, is adopted a broader-based, more egalitarian and individualistic Malayo-Muslim culture. One stimulus
for this, again reminiscent of the Protestant Ethic thesis,
is the relation of this reformist Muslim ethos to a rising
merchant class; their presence is revealed in the Congress
program, by numerous advertisements of their bookstores,
pharmacies, and cloth factories. One can envision in this
rather quiet period of the Muhammadijah, after the trials of
the time of Dahlan, a crystallization of a prosperous, efficient, and bourgeois life-style in the cozy Kauman, rendered
meaningful by a venerated, scripturalist religion promising
eternal salvation. Only the women remain subordinated, but
they are coming into their own.

Moving now to a more rapid and less circumstantial account of the ensuing years of the Muhammadijah, I shall sketch the growth, major organizational changes, and relation to the political epochs that brought the organization to its condition at the beginning of the seventies.

Growth and Organizational Development[1]

By 1930, the Muhammadijah had crystallized its functional divisions into these committees: *Tardjih* (a council issuing rulings as to what is acceptable in Islamic law); *Hikmah* (politics); *'Aisjijah* (women's affairs); *Pemuda* (youth organization); *Hizbul Wathan* (boy scouts); *Pengadaran dan Pendidikan* (education); *Taman Pustaka* (library and archives); *Tabligh* (celebrations and evangelism); P.K.U. *(Pembina Kesejahteraan Ummat* or social welfare and health care); *Ekonomi* (economic development of the organization); *Wakaf dan Kehartabendaan* (administration of property and resources of the organization).

Essentially these same functional divisions still held in 1970, though a significant change in locale had occurred. The more "worldly" committees (education, economics, politics, material resources, and health and social welfare) had moved to Djakarta, the national capital, in order to be closer to the hub of politics and bureaucracy. The archives, evangelism, law, women, and youth committees remained in the original headquarters of Jogjakarta.

The head of Muhammadijah is selected at a congress (Mu'tamar), which was held yearly from 1912 to 1940, only twice during the turbulent years of Indonesian occupation and revolution (1940-1950), and every three years since. After his selection, the head selects chairmen for each major committee. Since the death of K. H. A. Dahlan, the headship has been held by some dozen individuals. Their names need not be detailed here but certain cultural facts are noteworthy. All have been Javanese, and all but one (Mas Mansur, from Surabaja in East Java) have been from the vicinity of Jogjakarta, usually from the Kauman itself. All have been either businessmen or religious teachers by occupation and all have received primarily Islamic rather than government education, with perhaps some favoring of "old boys" from the Madrasah Mualimien, the premier Muhammadijah school in Jogjakarta. Until after World War II, these leaders had the patriarchial, polygynous, large families of the founders (Bagus, who ruled as recently as 1954, had 14

---

[1] For further information on Muhammadijah's development, see Salam (1965), Alfian (1970), Ali (1957), and Noer (1973).

children). In short, the socio-cultural base of the early
founders is expressed in drawing Muhammadijah leadership
largely from the Kauman community of the merchant-teacher
class and the Islamic schools.

Throughout its history, the appeal of Muhammadijah has been
largely urban, while its rival organization, traditionalist
Nahdatul Ulama (N.U.), has dominated the agrarian Javanese
countryside. A major source of Muhammadijah support has been
the merchants. In Jogjakarta in 1923, for example 1 percent
of the Muhammadijah income came from membership dues, 62 percent from miscellaneous sources such as subsidies, religious
tax, and business enterprises run by Muhammadijah, and 37
percent from donations by merchants. Alfian (1970, p. 319)
calculates that by 1932, donations from wealthy merchants
amounted to 176,847 guilders (probably equal to several million dollars today) in Jogjakarta alone.

Between 1912 and 1917, Muhammadijah was confined to the one
site at Jogjakarta, and in 1921 it had only five branches. By
1925 it had 25 branches, by 1942, 1275 branches, and by 1961,
524 major branches subdivided into 2216 minor branches. Membership increased from 4000 members in 1923 to 112,850 by
1937, and 159,000 by 1950. In 1970, Muhammadijah claims 2134
branches, more than 2500 subbranches, and a total membership
of six million, of whom over 459,000 have been enlisted in
the central organization.

While the organizational achievements of the Muhammadijah
are impressive, one may well follow the account of Solichin
Salam (1965) in singling out feminism and education as
two of its culturally noteworthy developments.

Derived from K. H. A. Dahlan's course for women, a women's
association named *Sapa Tresno* or "Those Who Love" was founded
in 1914. This maternalistic, Javanese name was soon changed
to the present activist, Arabic name of the women's branch of
Muhammadijah: 'Aisjijah, the name of an influential wife of
the Prophet. The objective of 'Aisjijah is to spread Islam
especially among women, and probably its most noteworthy
achievement has been the building of women's mosques and
prayerhouses—institutions allegedly unique to Indonesia.
Pijper (1934, p. 1) gave an eyewitness account of such a
mosque in Jogjakarta in the 1920s. It is a white building in
which an old woman beats the drum signaling that it is time
for prayer. Women enter in normal clothing though with the
head covered by a white cowl, and they cover themselves in a
cloak before beginning to worship. Every evening, between
the *al-magrib* and *al-isha* prayers, instruction in Islam is
given here for and by women. Itinerant female merchants use
the mosque as a place to lodge overnight. The first such
mosque was built by 'Aisjijah in the Kauman in 1922 (some say
1919), another was built in the Jogjakarta *santri* neighborhood

of Karang Kadjen in 1927, and subsequently many such buildings
were constructed throughout Java and Indonesia.

'Aisjijah also built numerous kindergartens, women's Islamic
schools, and by 1938 had mobilized some two thousand female
missionaries. Its energetic leader in 1970 was one of the
few female university professors in Indonesia, Professor Siti
Baroroh Baried, a "daughter of the Kauman" who is Professor of
Arabic and Dean of Arts at Gadjah Mada University in Jogjakarta.

Plate 2: Professor Siti Baroroh Baried, head of 'Aisjijah.

Solichin Salam (1965) regards Muhammadijah's most distinctive educational contribution as the moving of Islamic education beyond the traditional *pesantren*. In the *pesantren,* he
writes, the students either sat around the teacher and recited
from a text or listened passively to a lecture, whereas Muhammadijah introduced an emphasis on comprehension and reasoning
rather than memorization. Other innovations that Salam singles
out include instruction in Dutch language and secular subjects
to supplement the traditional study of Arabic language and religious subjects; character training to supplement the academic
and instill a sense of creativity, confidence, and responsi-
bility that replace the inferiority complex and egoism he sees
as deriving from colonialism; and Western-style apparatus,
such as violin, gramaphone, harmonica, checkers, and model
boats (which, according to my impressions, do not survive in
the present Muhammadijah schools).
   Throughout the history of Muhammadijah, the movement's
schools have been of two types: those parallel to the secular
government schools system, and those which are half secular
and half religious. During the Dutch period, Muhammadijah
had schools parallel to Dutch government schools at every
level from the elementary village school (*Volkscholen*) to the
gymnasium or secondary level. These were designated by the
Dutch labels but usually with the addendum "with the Qu'ran,"
indicating that some Qur'anic instruction supplemented the
secular. The half-and-half type, the *madrasah*, were founded
in Jogjakarta in 1923 as coeducational but had split by the
next year into the Madrashah Muallimaat Muhammadijah and the
Madrasah Muallimien Muhammadijah, for boys and girls respec-
tively. By 1939, there were 1744 schools run by Muhammadijah,
approximately one-half government-style and one-half *madrasah*-
style. The former were regarded favorably by at least some of
the Dutch officials, and were subsidized by the colonial government (Mailrapport 1925a).
   After the coming of Indonesian independence, the Muhammadijah kept its sexually segregated *madrasah* but transformed its
coeducational government-style schools into curricula and
levels consonant with those of the SD, SMP, and SMA (elementary, intermediate, and secondary) schools of the Republic.
Muhammadijah has also founded theological schools, religious-
teacher schools, technical schools, and a college.
   Muhammadijah's social activities are not, of course, restricted to women and schools. It has also established hundreds of clinics, and some pharmacies and orphanages throughout the archipelago. It publishes books, magazines, and
newspapers, and has organized labor unions, farming cooperatives, factories, and other instruments of development.

Plate 3:   Madrasah Muallimaat Muhammadijah, Jogjakarta.

Muhammadijah in Relation to Political Periods

The colonial period of the first quarter of the twentieth century was the time of Dahlan's leadership. During this period, the colonial government was making an effort to expand education for Indonesians. Dahlan's own educational endeavors contributed to this end and met with some governmental approval. Muhammadijans themselves recall the tenure of Dahlan as a time of creative and harmonious cooperation between the movement and the government.

During the 1920s and 1930s, the colonial government became concerned about the thrust of the numerous Indonesian movements toward national independence, so they tightened their control. None of the Muhammadijah leaders were exiled or imprisoned as were the radical nationalists and Communists, but Muhammadijah was affected by the so-called guru and wild school ordinances that restricted religious education and evangelism. Muhammadijans view this period as one of constriction on the life of the movement. Some of them (see, for example, the remarks of Djarnawi in Chapter Six) even consider the establishment in 1926 of the Nahdatul Ulama, the conservative, antireformist Muslim party, to have

been instigated by the Dutch to sabotage the growth of Muhammadijah.

Japan's occupation of Indonesia in 1942 brought an end to
Dutch colonial rule and initiated what the Muhammadijans and
other Indonesians term the Japanese Era. Muhammadijans see
this period as both negative and positive: negative in that
the disruption of life during occupation virtually stopped the
routine activities of the movement, but positive in that the
Japanese initiated the Muhammadijah leaders into national
politics. It was during this time that K. H. Mas Mansur, head
of Muhammadijah, joined the Japanese-instigated "four leaf
clover" of national leaders who represent major factions of
Indonesian life. The other leaders were Sukarno, a Javanese
nationalist, Hatta, a Sumatran nationalist, and Ki Hadjar
Dewantoro, a Javanese syncretist, and founder of Taman Siswa
schools.

The 1945 declaration of Indonesia's national independence
initiated the so-called Zaman Merdeka or Era of Freedom.
For Muhammadijah, this period was frustrating despite high
hopes at the start. After the declaration of independence,
Muhammadijah joined other Muslim groups in pressing for Indonesia to become a Muslim state. But only two Muslims, one
being the Muhammadijah leader Bagus Hadikusuma, were appoin-
ted to the Preparatory Committee which was charged with the
task of designing the government of the new nation, and no
Muhammadijah leader was included in the first cabinet. With
N.U. and other Muslim organizations, Muhammadijah formed the
very powerful Muslim party Masjumi, but this organization,
which opposed many of President Sukarno's policies, was banned
by Sukarno in 1960 when he created his Guided Democracy. By
the mid-1960s, the Communists were making huge gains in membership and influence, the reformist Muslims were deprived of
direct political action, and Muhammadijans lived in fear of
suffering the same ban as Masjumi.

Then in 1965-1966 fortunes turned abruptly. Sukarno was
toppled and the Communists massacred. Muhammadijah involvement in this military purge of their antitheist and anti-
capitalistic enemies varied from region to region, island to
island, and appears to have been fairly mild in the Jogjakarta area. Whatever their active involvement, however, the
Muhammadijans could not but greet with some relief the crush-
ing of the Communists and the demise of the syncretic Sukarno
who, though he had once briefly joined Muhammadijah while in
exile in Bengkulen, Sumatra, was disowned by the organization
after his death. (Thus they refused to honor a request he
had once made to be buried with the Muhammadijah flag on his
coffin.) The time seemed ripe for a Muslim revitalization.
Apparently recognizing the Muslim contribution, the government established so-called Mental Development Projects

throughout the country to educate the Communist prisoners in
Islam and thus bring them back into the fold. Muslim evangelism was stepped up with the establishment of various training centers to indoctrinate students and others in the techniques of missionary Islam (see D. Bakker 1970 and also the
description of a training camp in Chapter Six).

On the political front, many Muslims hoped to reestablish
the banned Masjumi, but this was not permitted by the Suharto
government. The compromise solution was the creation of a
new reformist party, the Partai Muslimin Indonesia or P.M.I.
(Indonesian Muslim Party), chaired by Djarnawi Hadjikusuma.
The P.M.I. was weaker than Masjumi basically for two reasons:
first, it was divided from the massive N.U. and, second, some
reformists considered P.M.I. a creation of the government and
would have preferred the oppositionalist Masjumi led by some
of the fiery old warhorses of that once-forceful organization.
Some Muhammadijans felt that the Muhammadijah should hew to
its long-standing policy of refraining from politics and thus
should limit its support for P.M.I. Given these difficulties,
it is not surprising that P.M.I. did poorly in the 1971 elections though, in fact, all of the parties did, and the only
victor was the central government organization, Golkar.

Plate 4: Djarnawi Hadikusuma, head of the Muslim Party of
Indonesia (on the right).

Muhammadijah's Accomplishments, 1923-1970

While this is not the place for an overall assessment of
Muhammadijah's achievements as an organization, the most obvious point is worth noting: Muhammadijah has grown and pro-
gressed during a period in which no comparable Indonesian
organization has even survived.

Since the death of K. H. A. Dahlan, the Indonesian nation
has experienced war, occupation, revolution, massacre, and
run-away inflation, all on the heels of a pre-World War II
depression that had already ruined many of the *santri* merchants who were the backbone of the Muhammadijah. Indonesian
government during this century has passed from Dutch colonialism to Japanese occupation to Sukarnoist "Guided Democracy"
to Suhartoist quasi-military rule. Each phase has seen the
banning or demise of some major organization. Of those
founded simultaneously with Muhammadijah—the syncretist Budi
Utomo, the elitist Indisch Partij, and the nationalist Sarekat
Islam—none even survived the colonial period. Of those
founded later than Muhammadijah, the Communist P.K.I., the
nationalist P.N.I., the progressive Islamic Masjumi, and the
conservative Islamic N.U., only N.U. was still viable after
the elections of 1971. Yet since its founding the Muhammadijah has steadily grown in membership while maintaining intact
its ideology and organizational structure.

What is the reason for this success of Muhammadijah? Most
obvious is its announced separation from politics. Though
certainly involved in politics at various levels, the organization has managed to place primacy on the fields of evangelism, welfare, and education, and has therefore avoided the
sting of government ban or election defeat. Nor has it been
tempted unduly by the rewards of power, as a result of which
its leadership has doubtless been the most selfless and least
corrupted of any major Indonesian-based organization. And,
finally, the relative lack of politicization itself reflects
the methodical, rational paradigm of Dahlan which has continued to guide the movement to the present day.

Aside from these evidences of organizational success, one
may assess the cultural development of the Muhammadijah based
on materials thus far presented. The rationalist, bourgeois
tendencies have been described, as reflected in the biography
of K. H. A. Dahlan and further in aspects of a congress held
after his death. While observation of similar congresses
today reveals much that is constant, there do indeed appear
significant developments in such realms as social hierarchy,
sexual roles, and regional traditions. By 1970, one sees no
Muhammadijah meetings held on the verandas of the nobility
and one meets no national leaders who bear the title of the
traditional, mystical teacher: *kijai.* Women are not now

seated behind screens, and they do not confine themselves to
shyly parroting speeches written by men. Indeed, the achievements of 'Aisjijah—their mosques, good works, organization—
are unique in the Muslim world. For both men and women, the
language of the public meeting has become almost entirely
Indonesian rather than Javanese or Arabic: the secular,
national language in place of either the language of the region or the religion.

Quite extraordinary is the Weberian-style rationalization
displayed by the women of 'Aisjijah who record their daily
activities and calculate the proportion of that time which
has been consumed by sin. These women are religious account-
ants, computing spiritual profit and loss. That this pattern
should appear among the women suggests an unusual degree of
initiative within 'Aisjijah and probably reflects the long-
standing prowess of Javanese women as merchants—their hard-
headed commercial attitudes are now transported to the religious sphere.

While Muhammadijah had already gone far in the purge of
syncretism by 1925, they have gone further since. No Imam
Bisri appears today. The reformist doctrine is apparently
too well established to need such a figure who blends Islam
with Javanism. And the competition of the traditionalist
Islamic school, the *pesantren*, has so faded from the Jogjakarta region that Hadjid's play would be meaningless in the
1970s.

CHAPTER FIVE

Muhammadijah Today: A Travelogue

On New Year's Eve, 1969, Indonesia's capital, Djakarta, was
enjoying a bawdy and lively celebration of the advent of the
1970s; rockets blazed from a display at the Monday Market,
while firecrackers exploded beneath the bare feet of pedi-cab
drivers, and wandering mobs sought pleasure. The revolutionary era of Sukarno had been puritanical by contrast. Where
Sukarno had banned Western dancing, discotheques now blared
rock music. Gambling had been legalized, transvestite male
prostitutes unionized, and Western pornographic films ("The
Seven Sins of Sexy Susan" and its sequel "Sexy Susan Sins
Again") were rife, replacing much of the Indonesian cinema
flourishing in the day of Sukarno. Lotteries, flashily-
dressed developers, Japanese banks, the collapse of the black
market, and a new expressway leading to the luxurious foreign
suburb of Kebajoran signalled a revival of economic as well
as sensuous aspects of Djakarta life.

In the midst of this Sodom and Gomorrah (as some reformists
saw it) on bustling Menteng Raya 62, is located the Djakarta
office of Muhammadijah. On the first working day after New
Year, I went there. Passing through a front room displaying
books on Islam and a middle room for prayer, I entered a back
room in which sat an efficient, energetic administrative secretary (male) in company with several members. I presented a
letter from the Indonesian Institute of Science (L.I.P.I.),
which explained that I had come to study the Muhammadijah.
While this announcement doubtless aroused concern, I was cor-
dially received and advised to visit each of several prominent
leaders in Djakarta, both to gain their approval and to hear

their opinions. These were Ir. H. Sanusi, chairman of the
national Muhammadijah committee on economics, Prof. H. Kasman
Singodimedjo, chairman of the committee on politics, Dr. H.
Kusnadi, chairman of the committee on health and welfare, and
the influential intellectuals, Hamka and Malik Ahmat.

Of the quintet, Ahmat most closely resembled the classical
santri model of Dahlan. Only he lived in a Kauman-like neighborhood and dressed in the *santri* shawl and cap. Of largely
Islamic education, he was born and raised in the Minangkabau
region of Sumatra. His specialty is theology (see the next
chapter for a summary of one of his lectures), and he is one
of the spiritual leaders of the Muhammadijah.

Sanusi gave an impression more like that of the secular officials and intelligentsia in the *orde baru*, the new Indonesia—an image which is consonant with the worldliness of his
"economic" function in the movement. A former Minister of
Industry, he resides in the elite suburb, Kebajoran, near the
new Muhammadijah university. Outside his house is posted a
guard, and in the driveway is parked a Landrover. Sanusi's
tan uniform resembles that worn by civilian as well as military organizers of the new emerging forces. He expounded
Muhammadijah objectives in the rhetoric of the five-year
plans: the movement must nationalize and internationalize,
consolidate at home and abroad, reeducate the Communists, and
develop its economic base. He is of Sundanese ethnicity and
Western-style education, through which he earned the title,
Engineer (Ir.).

Kasman Singodimedjo is a muscular, white-bearded, twinkly-
eyed Javanese orator whose voice crackles with resonance despite his 60 years of age. Asked to say something of his life
history, he stated simply, "I am a village person. I studied
on my own, but I have been a high official. I need say no
more." In fact, he has a Dutch education, a law degree, and
was a hero of the Masjumi party before its banning, and his
imprisonment, by Sukarno.

Kusnadi, of Madurese ethnicity, a smooth, courteous, quiet
physician, stated as his ideology: "I desire to improve the
society; this desire is like a poison as it spreads through
your system and absorbs your energies." Driving a Mercedes
automobile, he took me on a tour of Muhammadijah welfare facilities in Djakarta, including a maternity clinic, a new
Islamic hospital, and an orphanage.

Hamka, like Ahmat, is Minangkabau. He is a small, fair, bespectacled man of about sixty. The most popular *santri* writer,
he has authored novels, memoirs, philosophic and historical
tomes, and a biography of his charismatic reformist father,
Hadji Rasul. A renowned speaker, Hamka has travelled all
over the world. Seated on the porch of his neat stucco
bungalow near the new mosque in Kebajoran, he describes his

role in the movement today as cultural. Though his father
wanted him to become an Islamic teacher, he became instead an
author—still sticking, he says, to his dominant objective of
bringing Indonesians closer to Islam.

Quickly sketched, these five individuals exemplify the character of Muhammadijah in Djakarta. With the exception of Malik
Ahmat, they represent the worldly side of the movement—its
political, economic, welfare, and cultural emphases. They are
cosmopolitan, of varied ethnicity, and they resemble the modern Indonesian secular intelligentsia more than the traditional
Islamic teacher. Yet within the urban context of the capital,
they hew to the reformist tenets of the founder.

The Outer Branches

At the suggestion of the Djakarta office, I decided to tour
selected provincial and outer island branches of the Muhammadijah before returning for a period of longer observation in the
mother-city, Jogjakarta. For reasons of adventure, I travelled
by boat, "deck class," which meant sleeping on the deck for the
ten-day journey en route to Makassar, sharing a mat, plate, and
cup with a friendly group of Makassarese students from the
agricultural school at Bogor. After Makassar, I travelled by
plane to Minahasa, then again by boat to and from Ternate, returning from there to Makassar and then by various buses
through Java to Bali. From Bali I flew to Sumbawa Besar, on
the eastern side of Sumbawa. After a long wait in the company
of a Muhammadijan apostate en route to open a pornographic
movie house in Bima, I undertook with him an overnight trip
by boat to visit his family in that town on the western side
of Sumbawa. Stranded there as the malaria season and a flu
epidemic set in, I was able to catch a ride on a Landrover
driven along the jungle stream bed that served as a road back
to Sumbawa Besar. From Djakarta I flew to Padang and hopped
a bus up the winding road to Padang Pandjang, in the mountains
of Western Sumatra. Back in Java, I finally settled down in
Jogjakarta, the headquarters, where I spent most of the remainder of my field period; during this time I also visited various Muhammadijah branches at which I was invited to speak
(Tjilitjap, Surakarta, Pare, Pekadjangan) and several villages
where I participated in the movement's training camps.

Since space permits only the briefest report of these travels, only those features will be noted that express regional
variation on the reformist cultural theme. The map in Chapter
Two shows all places described.

Makassar. In this South Sulawesi (Celebes) port city the
reformist temper was most strikingly exemplified by the con-

trast between the bureaucratized life style of the Muhammadijah and the folksiness of the traditionalist party N.U. Muhammadijah provided extensive tours of well-organized schools, mosques, clinics and offices of the Muhammadijah, and numerous statistics and printed tracts. At the N.U. office, no one was on hand except the gregarious, local party head. He offered no tour, statistics, or printed material, but instead he invited me to a local *warong* (snack stand) to sample a brew of the regional-ethnic type, *soto Makassar*. While we sipped our brew, he talked about the need to sustain a "village feeling" and "village-style cooperativeness" within his traditionalist organization. He felt that retention of a certain amount of syncretic custom was better than the strict reformist purge. Asked about his own life history, he surprised me by beginning with a statement suggesting a time-concept like that of the Javanese *abangan*—that he did not know the year of his birth.

Ternate. Not food but architecture expresses the reformist/traditionalist opposition on this Moluccan spice island. Seat of an old sultanate (the palace remains, though the sultan is gone), Ternate boasts traditionalist mosques that are divided into two cross-cutting axes—a right/left division separating spiritual leaders from worldly leaders, and a back/front division separating nobles from commoners. Eschewing these dualistic expressions of syncretic cosmology, the reformists have built simple undivided mosques. They have also campaigned against mysticism, animism, Communism, and the traditionalist practice of gauging the date of the fast by watching the moon rather than by mathematical calculation. Yet, as in other provincial islands, reformist Islam on Ternate is also associated with such traditional Muslim patterns as patriarchy; in the house where I stayed, that of the bass-voiced head of the local reformist Indonesian Muslim party, the several brothers lived, ate, and prayed together while their wives kept to their own sphere. A certain humanitarianism and flexibility in relations between reformists and opponents was suggested by one bit of behavior: The head of Muhammadijah, a judge of the district court, employed as driver of his official vehicle (a truck that worked only in first gear) a man imprisoned for his Communism during the Gestapu conflict of 1965. By day, this trusty was bombarded with Muhammadijah evangelism from the judge as part of his effort at mental reconstruction of the Communists, and at night the prisoner slept in jail.

Bima. In this town on the remote and barren eastern side of the island of Sumbawa, a patriarchial pattern existed similar to that observed on Ternate many hundreds of miles away. Here

I lodged, first, in a household of merchant-brothers headed by
an Arab-featured old father whose hand was kissed by his sons
who reside on their joint property and jointly operate a business; second, in the home of a merchant-*hadji* who maintains
two wives.   Through features of language (e.g., the term *bini*
for wife) and networks of trade (e.g., links with the Arab
Alsagoff family of Singapore), the remote Bima society shows
closer links to the Islamized Malay peninsula than does the
geographically closer but culturally more distant Hinduized
Javanese society of Jogjakarta, and the Bimans are more rigidly orthodox, as in the covering of women in the street by
cloak and cowl.   Muhammadijans in Bima profess a radical anti-
Communism and anti-Sukarnoism (they speak proudly of the part
Bimans played in the attempt to assassinate him on Tjikini
Street in Djakarta).   The merchant-*hadji* states that Muslims
here join Muhammadijah because it "fits with rationality
(*akal*)," and he displays a linkage between the *akal*, the anal,
and the reformist impulse toward cleansing and purge: his
own personally designed commode features an inclined plane so
that feces disappear quickly rather than linger as in the
typical Indonesian apparatus.

Plate 5:   Main street of Bima.

Padang Pandjang. In this cool, mountain town of West Sumatra is located the most significant educational complex of Muhammadijah: the Mushalla Muhammadijah Kauman Padang Pandjang, known locally as the "Kompleks Kauman." Embracing all levels of schooling from elementary kindergarten to university, the Kompleks is organized along parallel tracks, the one more secular (government type), the other more religious (*madrasah* type); religious graduates include such luminaries as Malik Ahmad and Hamka. During my stay here (at the home of one of the ubiquitous *santri* merchant-backers of the movement), I was privileged to witness life in this Kompleks by attending initiation ceremonies for new students.

Held at night, the ceremonies were lit by lanterns that cast flickering shadows over the cowls and cloaks which completely covered the female students, who were seated separately from the males. Lasting a week, the ceremonies featured speeches by both male and female leaders who outlined the basic ideology of Muhammadijah, stressing that the important virtues of the movement are spiritual rather than material, and that they include simplicity, purity, faith in God, love of man, and the drive to reform the world in the image of the Qur'an. The week ended with drill and oath by the initiates and the crowning (by the anthropologist) of a student king and queen. Interesting in light of the theme of reformist concern with the careful organization of time was the great emphasis on outlining the agenda. Thus, on the final evening, the student leader announced, seriously: "The procession and the oath were preagenda. Now comes the agenda. First item on the agenda is the reading of items on the agenda."

In this center of reformist education, the contrast to traditionalism is most apparent in the schools. In the towns of Padang Pandjang and Bukit Tinggi are located the reformist Thawalib school, founded by the famous author Hamka's father, Hadji Rasul; a complex of schools still run by the family of Rasul's friend, Sjech Djambek; the Thawalib at Parabek attended by Hamka; and the reformist girl's school Dinijah Putri, founded by Rasul's pupil, the stern-faced Zainuddin Labai El-Junasi (see Plate 6). Teaching such subjects as theology, canonical law, scriptural exegesis, Arabic language, Islamic history, and the social sciences, the reformist curriculum is, according to one traditionalist teacher, nontraditional primarily in its emphasis on doctrine rather than scripture. Where the traditionalist schools (which are also rife in the region, frequently affiliated with PERTI, Persatuan Tarbijah Islamijah, the conservative Minangkabau organization akin to Java's N.U.) emphasize exegesis of the classical texts, the reformists bypass these symbolic forms and teach the moral and metaphysical ideas that they express.

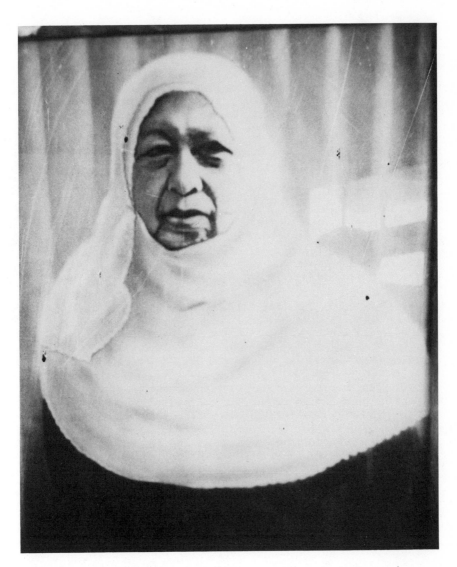

Plate 6: Zainuddin Labai El-Junusi, Founder of the Dinijiah
Puteri, Padang Pandjang.

   The reformist/traditionalist opposition would seem apparent,
also, in conceptions of the role of women, at least to judge
from impressions of one reformist and one traditionalist
school for girls. At the reformist Dinijah Putri, the cowled
and cloaked maidens are incarcerated in a Sumatran-gothic

Plate 7: Dormitory of the Dinijiah Puteri, Padang, Pandjang, showing moat and gate.

dormitory off-limits to male peers and separated from the town by a moat (see Plates 7 and 8). A female teacher gave this description:

We emphasize moral instruction, and we believe morality for a woman must be guarded constantly. So the girls must live in the dormitory which is constantly under guard. ...Their daily schedule is as follows: 4:30 A.M., wake up, bathe, get water for their prayer, pray; by 8 A.M. get ready for classes; 8-1, classes; 1:10 P.M., eat at the dormitory and then pray; 1 hour free for washing clothes; rest of the afternoon, study or nap; 6, dinner; 6:30, Magrib prayer; 7-9, read the Qur'an; 9, Issa prayer; 9:30, one-half hour free; 10 P.M., go to sleep. Our objective is to form women who have the Islamic spirit and who can become teacher-mothers who are active and responsible toward community and nation following the holy principles laid down by the blessed Allah.

Plate 8: Class in Session at the Dinijiah Puteri, Padang
Pandjang.

A traditionalist PERTI female *madrasah* is located in the
midst of rice fields only a few hundred yards from the Parabek
school of Hamka. As a Minangkabau comrade and I entered the
empty yard, the directoress burst out of the rattan center-
building and invited us inside, exclaiming that today was a
day of ceremony. Inside, a banner invitingly stated, "Welcome." As our eyes adjusted to the darkness of the large,
windowless room, we noticed that the back half was populated
by women, who turned out to be students, alumna, and students'
mothers. No males except for a few small boys and ourselves
were present. At the front, performances were being presented
by teen-age female students. They were dressed more attrac-
tively than the students of Dinijiah; in place of the cowl,
their long hair was topped by colorful scarfs, and in place of
the cloak they wore tight sarongs. After being invited by the
whispered word "Silahkan," each smiling girl would chant the
Qur'an or dance and sing lively Malay songs, accompanied by
the snapping of fingers and a rhythmic chant "Taq, taq...."
The stated objective of the directoress, which was less ascetic than that of the Dinijiah teacher, is to produce girls

who are charming, attractive, and marriageable.

Pekadjangan. If Padang Pandjang is the educational show-
place of Muhammadijah, the North Javanese village of Pekadjangan is the equivalent for economics. A village of some
eight thousand inhabitants, Pekadjangan is a major Indonesian
center for fabric manufacture and dying, and virtually all of
the villagers are reportedly members of Muhammadijah. They
form a cooperative which consolidates dyes, materials, and
labor and maintains a mechanized factory as well as many cottage industries. How all this began was explained to me by
a still-alert, bicycle-riding 81-year-old man who was one of
the catalysts:

Before 1924, the village consisted of thieves and murderers who were illiterate. I have been a *hadji* since
1970, before then I myself was a hoodlum. But then
came an Islamic teacher who preached that we would be
damned if we followed our old way. Fearing God, we
reformed. When Muhammadijah was founded, we joined.
Because our Pekadjangan Muhammadijah members were
thieves and murderers formerly, we did not fear disfa-
vor by society, and we kept on even when we were opposed by society. Luckily the head government official
here was a pupil of K. H. A. Dahlan, and he helped
Muhammadijah develop. Sarekat Islam (the Islamic
nationalist movement) tried to found a batik cooperative, but it had no laws, and it fell apart. But a
cooperative with Western-style laws could work. My
son learned Dutch in order to read the statutes!
Then we made a Dutch-language Muhammadijah school for
the children of the *hadjis* who were not allowed to go
to the regular Dutch schools. People here feared organizations like Muhammadijah since the Muslims were
[traditionally] not organized, and they thought that to
organize was to become Christian. But in 1934 the batik
cooperative was founded, and by 1936 it had begun to
truly advance because people saw the profit in it, and
also because textiles made in Holland were more expen-
sive than those made in Indonesia.

In 1970 the village of Pekadjangan appeared extremely prosperous by Indonesian standards, boasting large houses, Mercedes automobiles, television sets, refrigerators, and flush-
toilets. Every house seems to have at least one loom, and
these can be heard from dawn to dusk, working straight through
the normal Indonesian time of siesta. In addition to these
home looms, several hundred machines that weave, dye, and
press cloth are operated in the factories. Drawing funds

Plate 9:   In a textile factory of Pekadjangan.

from the industrial cooperative, the Muhammadijah schools
boast larger buildings than those of the government, and the
office building of this small branch is almost as big as the
national office (it also boasts the only automotive vehicle I
saw owned by any Muhammadijah office—a Toyota in which the
Pekadjangan delegates travelled to the training camp described
in the next chapter). Unlike most Indonesian villages, Pekadjangan is able to attract the return of its educated youth;
the headman has a degree in sociology, and the head of the
cooperative has a master's degree in economics from the University of Indonesia.
    Impression suggests that the Pekadjangan combination of
religious reformism and economic development has indeed modi-
fied traditional Javanese culture, which, however, has long
been less pronounced in this northern region than in the central Java rice plains. People scurry about, even slipping
under barriers at train crossings rather than wait for the
train to pass. They speak a less formal Javanese, and they
are allegedly not fond of the shadow plays, mystical cults,
and funeral ritual cycles adored by syncretists. Nor do they

like long speeches or long visits (a Muhammadijah official
from Semarang said that in Jogjakarta people are "sick at
heart" if he does not stay overnight, whereas here nobody
ever invites him). Much that is traditionally Javanese remains, however, according to my host; the practices that he
mentions are in the realm of child-rearing, such as carrying
the baby in the shawl, lending children to relatives, and
permitting boys to play with fighting cocks.

   Jogjakarta. Officially designated the "Special Region of
Jogjakarta," owing to its former status as a kingdom, this
central Javanese area includes some 1000 square miles, inhabited by over two million people, some 200,000 of whom live in
the city of Jogjakarta. Divided into four districts, each
with subdistricts which in turn are divided into villages and
hamlets, the rural area is administered separately from the
city. The city is divided into wards, such as Kauman, in
which originated Muhammadijah. Jogjakarta remains the national headquarters of the Muhammadijah.
   Capital of Muhammadijah, Jogjakarta is nonetheless a major
center of the syncretic culture. In Jogjakarta, the old syncretic sultanate of Mataram remains viable today. Though the
Sultan's palace has been partially converted into lecture
halls for the University of Gadjah Mada (named after the
Hindu-Java god-King), it remains a locus for syncretic civic
ritual. Thousands flock to the Sekaten fair on the palace
green, and the Garabeg ceremonies annually link the palace
to Islam through a ritual parade of a syncretic percussion
orchestra from the palace to the Great Mosque. Expressive of
a lively Javanism, mystical cults abound in Jogjakarta, as do
puppet play and dance performances, and manners are observably
more in accord with the Javanese ideal of civilized refinement
than in the provinces and ports.
   In Jogjakarta, then, one finds the full spectrum of Javanese
Islam, ranging from the reformist Muhammadijan to the deeply-
rooted and widely revered Hinduist, Buddhist, and animist
blend brought to smoothest perfection. This place of origin
of the most powerful anti-Javanist reform movement (Muhammadijah) is also the place of origin of the most powerful pro-
Javanist revitalization movements (Budi Utomo and Taman Siswa).
   The national office of Muhammadijah is near the center of
Jogjakarta housed in a two-story white building on 99 K. H. A.
Dahlan Street. This office faces out from the Kauman and
Kraton downtown, and Dahlan Street leads into the main business district which, though dominated by Chinese, boasts a
number of stores (mainly textile) owned by members of the Muhammadijah. The building contains a library, a distribution
center for literature, files of membership that go back to the
time of the Japanese occupation, workrooms for the Muhammadijah

Plate 10: A. R. Fahruddin, President of the Muhammadijah
(on the right).

magazine and bulletin, headquarters for the women and student
organizations, a prayer room, an auditorium, and a small
office for the administrator who oversees much of the local
and national operation, *Pak* Djindhar Tamimy. Here one meets,
too, the President of Muhammadijah, *Pak* H. A. R. Fahruddin,
and the President of 'Aisjijah, Professor Siti Baroroh Baried.
Those who drop by range from aged figures of the movement's
early history (e.g., Junus Anis) to youth leaders, and at one
time or another most of the active organizers throughout the
city and region will appear.
   Outside the central office are located the Muhammadijah
hospital, headed by the physician-husband of the head of
'Aisjijah, orphanages, schools, kindergartens, the Great
Mosque, small mosques, women's mosques, and the theological
faculty. Certain neighborhoods, such as Kauman and Karang
Kadjen, are full of Muhammadijah members and properties, such
as prayerhouses, kindergartens, and cottage industries.
Throughout the Jogjakarta Muhammadijah community, life is
organized around the five daily prayers, the Friday sermon,
the Fast, and most distinctively, evening study sessions.
Such study sessions are held by neighborhoods, youth groups,
women's organizations and other divisions within the Muslim

Plate 11:   The Muhammadijah National Office, Jogjakarta.

community. The format of the study session is not rigidly set
but consists essentially of lecture and discussion on some
topic concerning Islam, and the topics vary widely; indeed,
the subject of several sessions was my research concerning
Muhammadijah.

The other major institution of Muslim education in Jogjakarta is the school. In Jogjakarta, Muhammadijan boasts both
government and *madrasah* types of schools. The government-
style of schools provide study at the elementary, intermediate,
and secondary levels which can lead to university study, while
the religious schools lead to theological study at government
Islamic seminaries in Indonesia or Muslim universities abroad.
Muhammadijah also has kindergartens, normal schools, missionary schools, and other specialties. The total number of
Muhammadijah schools in Jogjakarta is 42, manned by 610 teachers and instructing 15,000 pupils.

Observation and questionnaire surveys of Muhammadijah schools
in comparison to the government ones (see Peacock, 1978) suggest that the Muhammadijah pupils come from more ethnically
heterogeneous backgrounds, that they are more ascetic, individualistic, more concerned with plans and future and tend
more to see life as a mission—all traits that logically link
to reformism. Among the Muhammadijan pupils, the reformist
traits are stronger in the religious schools than in the

Plate 12:   An 'Aisjijah Study Group, Jogjakarta.

government-style schools, and it is these *madrasah* that have
created leaders of the Jogjakarta Muhammadijah.

Patterns

Even a travelogue provides a sense of reformist pattern, in
opposition to traditionalist cultural contexts varying among
the different regions and islands. The basic reformist tenet—
purification of syncretic custom while holding strict allegiance to the Qur'an—and a certain asceticism and rationalization of life are found in guises ranging from the urbanized
intelligentsia of Djakarta to the polygynous merchant of Bima.
Everywhere, capitalistic merchants are the backbone of the
movement, and everywhere too, the strain of bourgeois life-
style is tempered by the Islamic value of patriarchy and a
restriction of the expressiveness, sexuality, and religious
participation of women. This latter pattern varies, however,
from the strict environs of Bima, where women are covered
with cloak and cowl, to the freer atmosphere of Jogjakarta
where women are clad in attractive blouses, sarongs, and
scarfs and have developed religious life in the women's
mosques and the activities of 'Aisjijah. In Sumatra, it ap-

Plate 13: A Muhammadijah student retreat near Jogjakarta.

pears that an intensive and activist women's reformism is
connected with an ascetic demeanor in comparison with a more
sensuous style for the traditionalist.

The syncretic culture, against which reformism is contrasted,
is common to all the islands, but varying in particular emphasis; in Ternate, it is exemplified in mosques arranged by
an archaic cosmology and hierarchy, in Java by animistic ceremonies and mystical cults. The syncretic folk culture is expressed also in such simple forms as traditional foods (*soto
Makassar* is paralleled by a type of *soto* or brew from virtually every island and region) and occasionally is linked to such
arch-enemies of reformism as the Communists. The reformist
impulse itself, while essentially the same everywhere in its
ideological and organizational basis, has its most noteworthy
economic expression in the textile industries of Pekadjangan
and Jogjakarta, its most noteworthy educational expression in
the schools of Minangkabau and Jogjakarta, its most noteworthy
organizational expression in Djakarta and Jogjakarta. As is
apparent, Jogjakarta remains the point of concentration of all
major features of the Muhammadijah; such befits the center.

Plate 14:   In a Muhammadijah kindergarten, Kauman, Jogjakarta.

CHAPTER SIX

Darol Arqom: A Muhammadijah Training Camp

Having traced cultural themes of the Muhammadijah biograph-
ically, historically, and geographically, we now encounter,
in some depth and first-hand, a Muhammadijah experience. In
the Muhammadijah training camp, many of the broad themes con-
verge: history of the movement, as recollected by the national leaders; features of organization, as taught by indoctrination instructors; ideals, as formulated by revered figures; and personal experiences, as narrated by participants.
Designed to teach the participant the essence of Muhammadijah,
the training camp so serves the participant-observer as well;
and readers, too, can share the experience of learning about
Muhammadijah as they pass vicariously through the major
phases of the camp.

Organized since the 1965-1966 purge of Communism, the so-
called Training Centers of Muhammadijah are designed to strengthen commitment and solidarity and to encourage the creation of
localized cadres after the Communist cell model. The camps
are organized in accord with stage of the life cycle and degree of socialization into the movement; the levels of the
four camps I attended ranged from teen-age to middle-age and
from neophyte to branch leader. Varying with level were
features of time, space, sex, and teaching. The lowest level
camps were less isolated temporally and spatially from society than were the higher level camps, less sexually segregated (they included both male and female while the higher
levels were single-sex), and more punitive in teaching
(teachers treated participants harshly, while higher level

ones treated them respectfully).[1] Despite such variation,
all of the training camps shared certain features, to wit:
isolation from normal, daily life spatially; continuous
absorption, without break or absence, into camp routine temporally; alternation between ideological instruction by
leaders and autobiographical confession by followers; and an
opening and closing ceremony. These basic features are shared
by indoctrination camps and initiation rituals around the
world, though, of course, given distinctive coloration by the
Muhammadijah.

The training camp to be considered here was the most advanced that I observed. It was called the T.C. (Training
Center) Darol Arqom, a name denoting friends of the Prophet
Muhammad, who met to prepare through discussion for the Islamic struggle. Lasting 15 days, the camp drew as participants 38 male Muhammadijah branch-leaders from throughout
Central Java.

The setting was a rural Muslim school, a quasi-*pesantren* in
a *santri* village within walking distance of a town halfway
between Jogjakarta and Surakarta. The school contained a
classroom used for all indoctrination lectures; an assembly
room that was the locale for holding opening and closing
ceremonies and at other times for the sleeping mats of the
branch-leader participants; a bedroom in which slept instructors, masters and lecturers; a row of outdoor bathrooms in
which one washed by splashing cold water from a basin; and an
outdoor area for eating. Participants prayed in the village
mosque, which was their only contact with village life.

The participants were all Javanese, through both mother and
father. They lived as far west and south as Tjilitjap, as far
north as Pekadjangan, and as far east as Magelang, all within
the central Java region. All but three were at least second-
generation inhabitants of central Java. Their ages ranged
from 20 to 49, the majority being between 30 and 39.

---

[1] This latter contrast is exemplified in the way the camps
wove the autobiographies of the individual into the indoctrination of the group. The lower levels had a so-called
"mental destruction" session where the person's life history was revealed through rude questions and subjected to
harsh criticism by instructors and peers. These sessions
were replaced at the higher levels by so-called "personal
introductions" where each person's narrated autobiography
was received courteously.

   Largely religious teachers and officials (only a few businesspeople) by occupation, most participants were graduates of the
government elementary school while a few had finished high
school.   None had a father who had gone beyond elementary
school or a father with a noble title—two facts which suggest
nonelite origins.   None had gone to the Jogjakarta Muallimien,
only half-a-dozen to other *madrasah*, and three to a *pesantren*,
and only a few had fathers with Islamic titles such as *Hadji*,
Imam, *Ustad*, *Kijai*, or *Modin*—facts which suggest a lack of
strong *santri* origins.   All were, of course, members of Muhammadijah, and about half also belonged or had belonged to such
Islamic political organizations as Masjumi.   In sum, the group
was ethnically Javanese, regionally central Javanese, socially
of neither pronounced *santri* nor elite background, but with
governmental education and employment.

Plate 15:   Physical Training at Darol Arqom.

Instructors, lecturers, and masters were, with one exception, Javanese, and they tended to be of higher social status than the participants. The head instructors were younger, but of higher education; the lecturers were older and of national rank in Muhammadijah; the masters were either older, wealthier, or of higher social rank.

Each day of camp began at 4 A.M. when everyone would awaken for the morning prayer. At 6 would be held physical training, including push-ups, knee-bends, jogs, and a kind of Javanese yoga. Then came badminton, bath, breakfast, and classes until noon. After the noon prayer we ate lunch (all meals consisted of rice, tea, a vegetable, and a bit of meat or fish), then came a nap, classes, dinner, and evening classes until approximately 11:30 P.M. with prayers punctuating at appropriate times.

Juxtaposed over this repetitive daily schedule was a progressive fifteen-day one in which events were ordered as follows:

Opening Assembly

Lecture on "Administration"—Daris Tamimy

Lecture on "Christology"—Soedibdjo Markoes

"Personal Introduction" (P.I.) #1

P.I. #2

"Terminology"—Amin Rais

P.I. #3

"History of the Islamic Struggle—Drs. Badruzzaman ["Drs." refers to the academic degree. "Doctorandus," equivalent to a Master's degree.]

"Rhetorica"—Mahmut Hamzah[2]

P.I. #4

P.I. #5

"Terminology"—Amin Rais

P.I. #6

Discussion A

Comments by Ahmad Azhar #1

P.I. #7

Comments by Ahmad Azhar #2

P.I. #8, #9, #10, #11

---

[2] Some names listed here are pseudonyms.

"ABC's of Christianity"—Soedibdjo Markoes

P.I. #12

Discussion B

Discussion C

"Principles of Muhammadijah"—Djindhar Tamimy

"Tauhid [Unity of God] I and II"—Malik Ahmad

"Politics I"—Djarnawi Hadikusuma

"Principles of Discussion"—Mahmut Hamzah

P.I. #13

"Politics II"—Djarnawi Hadikusuma

"Tauhid III"—Malik Ahmad

P.I. #14

"Tauhid IV"—Malik Ahmad

P.I. #15

P.I. #16

"Personality of Muhammadijah"—A. R. Fahruddin

"Administration"—Drs. Soewito

"Personality of Muhammadijah II"—A. R. Fahruddin

"Consciousness of Organization"—A. R. Fahruddin

General Discussion—Mahmut Hamzah

P.I. #17

"Social Research"—Drs. Sartono

"Tardjigh" [Islamic Law]—Drs. Sartono

Discussion

P.I. #18

Fieldtrip

Closing Assembly

These events will be summarized in an order reflecting what seems to have been the logic of the camp experience. The opening and closing ceremonies were the entrance and the exit to the experience. The major events were the lectures, which are categorized along a continuum running from principles to practice, culminating in a fieldtrip. Sandwiched between lectures were the autobiographical Personal Introductions by participants. For brevity and coherence, the material will

be divided according to these categories[3] though the reader
can reconstruct the chronology by referring to the sequence
above.

The language used in all instances was Indonesian.

Opening Ceremony

This event was held in the evening in the assembly room,
where we were not to meet again until the closing ceremony.
After an Islamic salute and response, we heard a welcome address by one of the three young camp instructors, the 29-year-
old Soedibdjo. Of Catholic and syncretic background, he is an
advanced medical student who converted to Islam while in
medical school and has become one of Muhammadijah's most outspoken analysts and critics of Christianity. His points
tonight include a variation on one made by Hadjid at the 1925
Congress: Christian doctrine is irrational (in its polytheism)
yet its practice is effective (in social welfare), so Muslims
should learn from the practice while retaining their own belief.

Following Soedibdjo, a former regional leader, Dursono, expresses regret that he is retiring in order to move to Djakarta. He gives a gentle Javanese-style talk explaining that both
sabar (patience) and *ichlas* (stoic dedication) are needed for
the struggle and he gives his new home address while inviting
all to visit him. (Note that the virtues Dursono praises
[*sabar* and *ichlas*] are the same Javanese ones attributed to
K. H. A. Dahlan; it is these which are also in the handbook
for Darol Arqom and, indeed, define a Javanese core beneath
the Islamic layers of the Muhammadijah.)

The last speaker to preside is the instructor, Amin Rais,
who is a smooth, articulate University of Gadjah Mada lecturer

---

[3] *The Buku Pegangan Untuk Instruktor Darol Arqom Tingkat
Wilajah* (Handbook for Instructors in Darol Arqom at the
Regional Level) categorizes the curriculum as follows:
first "ideology," which subsumes Tauhid and the Principles and Personality of Muhammadijah; second, "theoretical knowledge," which takes a more objective vantage
point than ideology and includes the History of the
Islamic Struggle, Comparative Religion (including the
Study of Christianity), Comparative Organization, Terminology, and Leadership; third, "Practical Application,"
which includes administration and social research;
fourth, "Field Study." Neither personal introductions
nor opening and closing ceremonies are mentioned in the
handbook, which confirms that these events serve to frame
and fill the formal curriculum.

married to the daughter of a batik manufacturer who is serving
the camp as a master. After cutting short a protest from a
fiery branch-leader concerning the method of selecting the
leader of the prayers, Amin outlines certain rules of the camp
(e.g., no absences permitted), and the company retires.

Lectures

Tauhid (The Unity of God). Malik Ahmad, the Minangkabau
teacher and theologian from Djakarta (see Chapter Five) is
said to be spiritually inspiring, and of all speakers he comes
closest to revealing the mystical, emotional basis of the movement. In this he resembles such Minangkabau forebears as
Rasul, while the Javanese lecturers resemble Dahlan and other
Javanese figures of the movement in focusing on organization,
history, and propriety. Malik is the only non-Javanese in
the camp, and his singularity of ethnicity perhaps heightens
the spirituality and purity of his lecture—which concerns that
which transcends all differentiated substance (including the
social, which includes the ethnic), i.e., *Tauhid*.
  Malik describes God as a source of energy, like electricity.
This energy, which derives from God's undifferentiated unity,
his *Tauhid*, illuminates everything—one's wife, handkerchief,
manners, and even the drinking glass before him which has divine essence. This *Tauhid* enters man as if it were a sperm
from Allah that takes His shape inside the human soul.
  What is evil is to attend to that which does not partake of
Tauhid, that which is differentiated: the syncretic shrines
and charms, lust, and gambling or sport. Lack of faith in
God has led to the collapse of the West and the rise of Communism. Even the Muhammadijah movement can survive only insofar
as it flows from God.
  After Malik's lectures, he is asked many questions, e.g.,
how to prove God's existence (Malik replies that prayer which
gets results is proof); whether he believes in the existence
of spirits such as genies and devils (he says that although
these are now known only spiritually, someday we shall see
them materially); whether one can believe in mystics and
shamans (he says sometimes they can indeed cure); and questions about the after-life and the punishment of infidels.
Concerns expressed to Malik center around the unseen, the
spiritual, and its mysteries.

Agama Perbandingan (Comparative Religion). Where Malik
lays bare the spiritual root of Islam, the speakers on comparative religion treat doctrinal contrasts between Islam and
Christianity; in terms of the categories laid out by the
Darol Arqom handbook, Malik treats ideology (root doctrine)
while the comparative perspective provides theoretical

knowledge. One speaker, a professor at the government Islamic seminary in Jogjakarta, is quite analytical while the former Catholic, Soedibdjo, is more polemical (in this sense, ideological).

Soedibdjo lights into abuses of the West, such as racism, divorce, suicide, and alcoholism. In response to a question as to whether Toynbee said Islam will someday rule the West, he replies that Toynbee says only Islam can save the West from destruction. He castigates the spiritual bankruptcy of the Church, and he quotes the Austrian convert to Islam, Leopold Weis, to the effect that Freud and Marx lie behind Western hatred of Islam.

The professor criticizes such apologetics (without direct reference to Soedibdjo) saying that it is strange that Islam acts like a persecuted minority when in fact it is a majority. (Later, Soedibdjo, in indirect rebuttal of this indirect criticism of himself, notes that although Muslims may be in the majority in Indonesia they are opposed in the world as a whole by large and aggressive populations such as the Christians.)

Mocking the term "T.C." (acronym for Training Center), the professor rasps it in a nasal tone (this pronunciation is imitated in the barracks from then on). Now he criticizes those who consider it essential that an Islamic society already be Islamic in every way in order to term such a society "Islamic"; the important thing is that it be *striving* toward that ideal.

He considers reformist rebellion against the scholastic schools of Muslim law as parallel to Christian rebellion against dominance by the church; but he contrasts the place of the Bible in Christianity with that of the Qur'an in Islam. To criticize logical or factual contradictions in the biblical text by saying, "This doesn't fit with reason" is irrelevant; Christianity doesn't rise or fall with the consistency of the Bible but with faith in Jesus.

He condemns secularism and pragmatism, as in the reformist reduction of sacred ritual to pragmatics: "fasting is for dieting, ablution is for hygiene, and prayer is for exercise." No, ritual is first of all spiritual.

Remarks relevant to this and other topics are given by Ahmad Azhar, head of the Committee for Guidance of the Young Generation, which oversees the youth activities of the Muhammadijah, and Dean of the F.I.A.D., a missionary training school for Muhammadijah. Educated at Al-Azhar University in Cairo, Azhar is a dynamic, articulate, muscular person who, before zooming off on the back of the batik-manufacturer master's motorcycle, speaks on the perils of fetishism. When he describes the shrines of Iraq and the worship of the Prophet's hair in Pakistan, participants murmur, "tsk, tsk, tsk," and exclaim, "My God."

The Islamic Struggle and Islamic Ritual. Drs. Badruzzaman, a husky, bass-voiced, bespectacled principal of the school at which the camp is held, traces the history of Indonesian Islam from the mystic to the reformist, whom he terms the prophetic teacher who dares oppose anyone in the name of truth. He also makes the only biographical mention of Muhammad that I noted during the camp: "Muhammad was born, traded, married, meditated, had his revelation, and became leader of the Arabs, then master of the world. Is it possible that an ordinary man could do all this? No. The blessed Prophet was sacred."

Lecturing on Islamic ritual, Badruzzaman describes each step in ablution and its meaning. Participants then ask questions: Must one bathe after excretion? Should a woman let her long hair down for ablution? The questions resemble similar ones heard at other gatherings: How is purity insured by ablution after ejaculation, erotic dreams, menstruation? There is much concern for ritual purity.

Turning from Islamic topics in general, we consider now those lectures that deal with the Muhammadijah itself. The two major speakers here were the leaders of the two major reformist Muslim organizations in Indonesia: *Pak* (Father) A. R. Fahruddin, President of Muhammadijah, and Djarnawi, head of the Muslim Party of Indonesia (P.M.I.). As will be seen, these two speakers took complementary points of view.

Muhammadijah. A. R. Fahruddin was born in 1916 in a village near Jogjakarta. He graduated from a Muhammadijah elementary school in 1928, then a Muhammadijah teacher's school in 1934. After teaching in Palembang, Sumatra from 1934 to 1944, he returned to Jogjakarta to live in his natal village and teach in a Muhammadijah school until 1947, at which time he became an official within the Department of Religion; he now heads the Jogjakarta division of information within that Department, in addition to heading Muhammadijah (it is the government post that provides his salary). His father taught in a *pesantren*; his own children have followed *Pak* A. R. in getting their education in Muhammadijah schools, and two are now enrolled in the Jogjakarta government Islamic seminary (I.A.I.N.). *Pak* A. R. is a heavy-set, bespectacled, warm, humorous man who, unlike some of the younger figures of the movement, affects no uniform. Instead, he wears sandals, baggy pants, and a shirt hanging outside. After riding a rickety bus from his small house in the Kauman to the camp, he is now found sitting in his sarong drinking coffee with "the boys" in seeming contentment. *Pak* A. R.'s lifetime of education and service in reformism has not removed his distinctively Javanese flair for immediately establishing a social bond of spiritual and personal depth and warmth, and he is much liked by the T.C. participants.

Pak A. R. approaches the topic of Muhammadijah's "Personality" historically and anecdotally, deviating altogether from the abstract outline of principles that the Darol Arqom handbook suggests as the substance of the lecture "Personality of Muhammadijah." *Pak* A. R. sketches the flavor and character of each leader and his administration. Dahlan and his successor K. H. Ibrahim served the phase of creation and formation. Hasjim took over and, like Dahlan, was industrious and orderly; "Unlike me, he did not waste time joking and telling stories." K. H. Mansur who served from 1937 to 1942 was knowledgeable in religion and powerful in debate, and his devotion to the cause was demonstrated once by his continuing to speak at a certain assembly right after receiving the news that his own mother had just died. Bagus held the movement together during the occupation and into the period of independence, and it is entirely unjust to accuse him of collaboration with the Japanese, as some have done owing to his diplomacy regarding them. Bagus' successor was brusque and would tell Communists point blank they were headed for Hell. *Pak* A. R. proceeds in this way to give an anecdotal history of the leaders up to 1968, when K. H. Faki Usman became president. *Pak* A. R. affectionately imitates Faki's lisp and quotes his witticisms, then mentions Faki's premature death. *Pak* A. R. tactfully excludes mention of his own succession to the presidency, which was to replace Faki Usman.

In the old days, says *Pak* A. R., we felt respect for a leader, but today—everybody's just casual (he illustrates by mumbling something disrespectful in low Javanese). Our present leaders include Kasman Singadimedjo (He's old but strong as a horse; he never stops travelling and speaking.); Malik Ahmat (He's sick more often than well.). For literature, we have Hamka; for knowledge, Rasjidi (a religion professor); for health, Kusnadi. "What about money?" asks a soldier participant. "Sanusi," (head of the economics committee; see Chapter Five), responds *Pak* A. R. "Anyway, if it really gets tight, you can use your uniform." He mocks the train conductor asking for tickets, the soldier answering, lisping "Shushah" (times are hard) and using his military privilege to avoid paying. This turns out to be, in fact, exactly what happened en route to T.C. as the soldier reveals later in his Personal Introduction; *Pak* A. R. reveals his awareness of the common plight. Then he goes on to explain how Muhammadijah's main function is evangelism: *da'wah*.

In his second lecture on the "Personality of Muhammadijah," *Pak* A. R. begins by making fun of those who care about clothes: wear a towel on your head if you want to look like a *kijai* (old fashioned Islamic teacher, who wore a turban)—what matters is doing *da'wah*. Continuing, he describes the debates that have raged over whether Muhammadijah should be politicized, but now the movement has revived to do *da'wah*. Who guides it?

"Allah," all participants chorus. *Pak* A. R. here emphasizes
that God, not a political leader, is the ultimate authority.

Pak A. R. begins his third lecture by quoting a proverb in
Javanese, *"legan golek momongan; nganggur golek gawejan"* (The
childless woman seeks a child to care for, the jobless man
seeks work). That's Muhammadijah, it must be active. Then
he turns again to the theme of politicization and argues that
activism need not involve politics.

Politics. While *Pak* A. R. held no overt debate with Djarnawi Hadikusuma, A. R.'s antipoliticization lectures did follow the speeches of this head of P.M.I., and they likely were
intended to qualify Djarnawi's apparent pro-politicization
stance as well as outbursts of several other participants; as
Chapter Four notes, the issue of whether Muhammadijah should
become a political party has been decided negatively throughout its history.

Djarnawi's father, Bagus, was president of Muhammadijah,
1945-1950. Like *Pak* A. R., Djarnawi is a Jogjakartan, and
he attended Muhammadijah schools from elementary through
teacher's college. He then taught until the late 1940s, when
he joined the revolutionary army as a lieutenant, fought, and
was wounded. Returning to Jogjakarta and to teaching in 1949,
he remained there until moving to Djakarta in 1970 to organize
the campaign of the P.M.I. Under the name D. Kusuma, he has
written five novels and has also published Muhammadijah books
on Christology. Less fatherly than *Pak* A. R., he is a small,
feisty, crackling-voiced polemicist with humor.

Djarnawi begins his lectures on "Politics" by making an
analogy between comparative religion and comparative politics,
both of which lead to insight. Insight into organization is
necessary since Allah has decreed that things be organized.
Praying must be organized, likewise missionary activity, even
Nallo and Buntul (the lotteries), pickpockets, and (his voice
rises, evoking laughter), even prostitutes....

Djarnawi begins tracing the history of Islamic organization
in Indonesia up to the debut of Muhammadijah's rival, the
conservative Nahdatul Ulama, or N.U. (laughter when he says,
"Then came N.U."). He quotes an "American lady researcher"
as asking him, "'Was N.U. created by the Dutch to ruin Muhammadijah?' I replied, 'Perhaps.'" He explains how N.U.'s
traditionalist ideas were effectively perpetuated by its modern organization.

In his second lecture, Djarnawi begins by saying that it is
true that Muhammadijah is not a political organization. But
neither is it an educational or social organization. However,
it has an educational aspect, a social aspect, and it is
"ber-r-r-r-r-politik" (politicized)!" From the first it has
been so. Pijper, then the Dutch advisor on Islamic affairs,
once asked a Muhammadijan: "Why does Muhammadijah mix in

affairs of the state?" To which the Muhammadijan replied,
"Why does the state mix in affairs of Muhammadijah?"

He relates how when Muhammadijah was part of Masjumi it
could only pay taxes but not hold office, for it was not officially political. In 1966, they tried to revitalize the Masjumi but were not allowed to, and so they formed the P.M.I.
He goes on to say that P.M.I. has no direct relation to
Muhammadijah, but is spawned by it as father to child. And
in the up-coming election the child needs the father's support: a million votes.

Organizational Principles. More introverted than *Pak* A. R.
or Djarnawi, *Pak* Djindhar Tamimy is bespectacled and stout,
the efficient administrator of day-to-day organization of the
movement and formulator of a document entitled, "The Fundamental Principles of Muhammadijah." This is the topic of his
lecture. Unpaid for his full-time job with the movement
(which he deems sacred service), he lives in a modest house
and supports his family through small trade by himself and
his wife, who is a relative of the head of 'Aijsijah, Professor Siti Baroroh Baried.

Pak Djindhar's lecture does not repeat the principles,
which have been published, but simply comments on a few
troublesome points. These include, the extent to which mystical feeling and aesthetic form should enter into the organizational life; whether banking is to be permitted (given the
Islamic taboo against drawing interest); what should be the
relation of movement to village? The basic point, he says,
is that the struggle should be carried out in line with the
five-fold philosophy of the Indonesian state (formulated in
a document, Pahtjasila) and in emulation of Muhammad.

The brother of *Pak* Djindhar, Daris Tamimy, speaks on "Administration," expressing visually and verbally his image of
Muhammadijah as a movement. It *is* a movement *(gerakan)*, it
must progress *(madju)* toward a goal *(tudjuan)*, and therefore
have a plan *(rentjana)*, but in accord with Islamic morality.
He chalks on the blackboard what he terms the forward movement *(bergerak madju)* as an ongoing spiral, which he contrasts
with circles. The movement's dynamism *(dinamis)* he represents
as a horizontal, straight arrow; the movement must not decline,
which he represents as a bent arrow pointing downward. Then
he diagrams the organization as a segmentary system—a big
square composed of smaller squares within squares that represent the branches and subbranches. What is of interest in
this presentation is the extent to which Darul's visual image
corresponds in broad contours with conceptions of movement
and organization that Western thinkers such as Weber customari-
ly term rational; the verbal conception of Muhammadijah em-
braces the rational, as Daris shows by his terminology, and
apparently this conception penetrates to visual imagery too.

Younger figures in the movement lecture on additional principles of organization. Drs. Sartono thus speaks on "Method
of Social Research," outlining basic methods of formulating
hypotheses and collecting data, then showing, without great
enthusiasm, how they could be applied in problem-solving for
Muhammadijah. One of these younger speakers, dressed in a
uniform, punctuates each point by actually saying, "Now we
pass to the matter of B" (or C, D, etc.). The younger speaker
thus verbally and literally follows the numbered and lettered
outline of the printed handbook. A Djarnawi or a Fahruddin
throws the book away and uses an anecdotal style that leaves
the outline implicit in the narrative. Participants gave
the opinion that these younger figures were less inspiring
than the "fathers" of the movement, whose lectures more
closely resembled the traditional Islamic style of sermons,
stories, and speeches. But in their own discussions the
participants themselves were infected by the Western notions
of management-training, and they used the jargon and outlines
of the bureaucratic report.

Personal Introductions

During time not occupied by lecture, 23 of the 38 participants were called to the front of the group to give a Personal Introduction. Form and content were left up to the
participant; each gave a routine account of his birthdate,
schooling, and work, followed by whatever additional personal information each chose to provide spontaneously or in
response to questions from the participants. To give a flavor
of these "introductions," the first eleven will be summarized
individually after which major themes in the remaining dozen
will be noted.
Number 1 begins by saying, "If you look at my age as revealed by gray hairs, you can see that I am the same age as
Pak Paidjo" (a large, somewhat older person called *Pak Lurah*
[Father Headman] to indicate his leadership of the community
of trainees). A participant asks when he will marry. He
replies, "Up to me," and another asks,"Do you fear marriage?"
He replies, "Not yet, just that I don't desire to marry yet."
Number 2 is greeted by laughter when he stands; he is the
camp clown. He says he was born in 1942, he has only an
elementary school education, his career at present is in the
Department of Religion. His father and father-in-law are
modin (Muslim officials) a remark which evokes laughter
(apparently owing to the rustic conservative image of the
modin) and the teasing question: "Do you want to be a *modin*,
too?"
Number 3 is the *Pak Lurah*, who says he is head of Muhammadijah in a certain village. He is employed in sawmilling. His

wife is a graduate of the Muallimaat (the Jogjakarta girl's
madrasah), and she has been secretary in 'Aisjijah since 1956.
He has been in Muhammadijah since 1959. A gentle harmonizer
who speaks in a slow, ponderous voice, *Pak Lurah* confesses a
mild lapse from camp discipline: "Just recently I heard a
song on the radio which aroused my yearning for wife and child,
and that is not fitting in a Muhammadijah cadre."

Number 4 is an outspoken bespectacled man who is termed
"hot" by other participants. He says he will divide his account into three categories: family, education, and struggle.
To begin, he tells the names of his children in order of
birth, then he says an aim in life is that each become a
protege of some personage, for example, Djarnawi or Peacock.
He then recounts that he was educated in the Pondok Moderen
at Gontor (a reformist adaptation of the traditional Muslim
school), and that he works in a government business which is
about to fail, after which he will move into private business.
His wife was Christian, as was his father-in-law. His wife
was formerly secretary of a Christian women's movement, but
is now head of an 'Aisjijah chapter. He himself got as far
as a university but did not finish. He has had various offices in the Muhammadijah, and he likes to sing. He says that
his older brother once killed someone, apparently for religious reasons, and later he discovered that the brother had
killed a man who threatened to kill his father; it is best
not to know such a thing for it would cause one to mix religious motives with the personal.

Number 5 states that, like many villagers, he remembers
only the day, not the year that he was born. He is from an
abangan family which did not do prayers, but he himself always wanted to. Now, praise be to God, he is a Muhammadijan.
(The participants chorus, "Praise be to God.") He tells of
being one of a group of Muhammadijah youths who resisted and
finally stopped a mystical movement that "threatened the
safety of our society." Participants ask him how many wives
he has; he replies: "One," and what his hobbies are: he
replies, "Badminton and evangelism."

Number 6 is a soldier from Supara, born in 1934. He remarks
that his wife married young because she wanted to, not because
she had to. She is "sweet brown" in color, he remarks fondly,
and he taught her to know religion. His five children were
each given a "good name" and one who was sick has recovered
(apparently reflecting the syncretist belief that the goodness
of the name determines the welfare of a child). He joined
Muhammadijah in 1965, he has worked constantly performing
evangelism, and he used his uniform to obtain free passage to
the T.C. (Everyone laughs at this.)

Number 7 says he entered Muhammadijah when he was small.
He tells of his education, both in a government school and a

madrasah. Now he is a merchant, he enjoys travel. His wife
is five years older than he. A participant asks how the marriage came about, and he replies, "She was active in 'Aisjijah,
I in Muhammadijah." A participant comments: "Because you are
supported by your wife (possibly referring to her older age
as well as to her role in 'Aisjijah), you can truly move [in
the movement], then when you are tired, you can quickly fall
asleep."

Number 8 was born in 1929, he had no training in religion,
he was a school teacher. He graduated from the teacher's
normal school in 1943, married in 1955, is father of six
children. His father, a Muhammadijah head, struggled in the
movement, was arrested by the police, and has never been
found. A sinewy, lean person who sometimes leads the morning
physical training in spite of the fact that he is 41-years-old,
Number 8 spent three months in the corps of Darul Islam (a
West Java movement), and in 1947, he also underwent training
in the paramilitary Hizbullah. In 1963, he moved to Pekadjangan (where I met him again a month later, witnessing his
role as a respected and dedicated subordinate leader in that
branch of Muhammadijah).

Number 9 tells that his wife is of Arab descent, from a
group in Borneo which so violently opposed his marriage to
her that she cannot return home owing to the position of a
certain uncle.

Number 10 relates that he was born in the midst of a N.U.
milieu. He was educated in a *madrasah,* but after he supported
the views of his teacher his family rejected him, so he joined
the Muhammadijah. His family wanted to arrange a marriage for
him, but he refused and then, without their knowledge, married
his sweetheart. To this day, he says, "I love Muhammadijah."

Number 11 says that he was born in either 1937 or 1938, his
father and father-in-law being N.U. "Don't laugh," he requests.
"There were five children, including me. Praise God, none of
them became N.U." He attended a *pesantren,* but learned nothing: "I just enjoyed going fishing. I became friends with a
—pardon me for saying it—Christian priest. At 25, I married,
thinking that when I'm 40, the first child will be in junior
high school. After 11 months, we had the first child. Now I
am a religious teacher. The head of my school is N.U., and I
was not given his permission to come here. Once I received a
suggestion that I leave the P.I.; to this day my parents are
N.U. Since 1962, I have been secretary of several Muhammadijah committees and my wife was a secretary of 'Aisjijah."

The remaining dozen accounts include the several descriptions of conversion to Muhammadijah from syncretic upbringing.
For example, Number 14 recounts,

Although my parents were pious, I myself was a Hinduist

syncretist. I was evangelized, but with no result. Finally, I dared to marry in order to achieve calmness of
heart, then I joined Muhammadijah and took over leadership of a certain branch.... [He does not recount how
he converted from syncretism to Muhammadijah.]

Others tell of conversion from N.U.:

My family is N.U. and they practice mysticism. When I
accepted an appointment in the government Religious
Affairs office, they asked me how I could do so without
being able to lead the Berzandji [the traditional chant
celebrating the birth of Muhammad, normally done by N.U.
but not Muhammadijah].

One tells of coming from a family where all of his brothers
are Communists:

The reason is that my mother was so poor that she had
to lend her children to be raised by others, so that
they were not properly trained in religion. My older
brother and I do not agree concerning ideology, to the
point that he feels that every prayer is like a sin.
[He weeps slightly upon saying this; participants explained that they thought it was because he remembered
his mother's poverty, not because his brother had entered the P.K.I. or because of the problem of the meaning of the prayers.]

Additional accounts, too, comment on the opposition between
Muhammadijah and the rival movements, especially how one has
avoided temptation to join them despite being raised or now
living in the midst of them. One man speaks of owning a
store in a syncretist-Communist neighborhood, another says
that he lives at a shrine which is a center of syncretist and
Communist activity, and another recounts how he helped smash
a Communist youth group when he was a member of the N.U. youth
movement, Ansor.
Aside from the theme of contrast between Muhammadijah and
rival movements, other themes common to the remaining accounts
are family life—how many children one has, what one's wife
does—and career history: one man, for example, tells how he
has made a career of manufacturing a certain hot sauce and he
puts in a plug for his product in case any of the members
should wish to purchase such a sauce before leaving on the
pilgrimage.

Discussions

Held at intervals during the agenda, the so-called discussions centered around issues such as the form of discussion (how to carry on a discussion, what sort of report of the discussion should be made), should Muhammadijah be politicized, how a cadre is built, and whether Muhammadijah should institute a research bureau (some jokingly suggested I was that). In lectures and personal introductions, the speaker stood at the front of the room facing the participants in rows, but for discussion the chairs were arranged in the shape of a wedge with a leader at the center table, suggesting that the discussions were less directed than lectures, but still leader-centered.   For example, the "hot" person, Number 4, harangues that Muhammadijah should be more politicized, to which the cool leader, Ahmin Rais, replies, "Thanks to Number 4 for his analysis that was long and deep and smacked of politics," and then passes smoothly to another topic.

When these discussion groups broke into smaller, participant-led subunits of ten or so persons, conversation became animated and lengthy.   The most striking quality of talk was the emphasis on *istilah* (terminology) for the labelling of categories of organization.   There was much discussion of whether the Bureau of Research should have "internal" and "external" aspects, the importance of distinguishing clearly between "policy planning" and "performance," and discussion at length of other abstract management categories.   Participants were concerned, too, with the proper labelling of units of curriculum, and one of the major recommendations to come out of their discussion was that the term "social psychology" be used in place of *ilmiah da'wah* (the knowledge of evangelism) to designate communications study.   All of this reflects a pattern appearing elsewhere in Indonesian life, a great concern with ordering through abstract labelling; old cosmological classificatory concerns shine through the management jargon and organizational pragmatism.

Conversation

During the early afternoon nap-time and late at night after classes, participants would relax in their quarters by donning sarongs, lounging about on each other's beds or mats, and drinking coffee.   Listening to the Thomas Cup badminton tournament broadcast from Kuala Lumpur, they cheered when Indonesia shut out Canada; the behavior of these Javanese males in relation to their national sport was very much like that of American men watching football on television or British and Dutch spectators at a soccer match.

Plate 16:   A coffee break at Darol Arqom.

   Rarely did the participants discuss doctrine or theology,
though they gossiped about the personalities of leaders.
Doubtless owing to the all-male, boot-camp isolation, sex was
also a topic. One participant stated openly that he found it
hard to be separated from relations with his wife and wondered
how I could endure lengthy separation from mine. Seemingly
in answer to this query, another expounded his theory of
sexuality in Java versus the West, which equated the hot,
tropical climate and fertile soil with the hot sexuality and
high birthrate of the Javanese, by contrast to the cold climate, barren soil, cold sexuality, and, therefore, low birthrate of the West. On the final day of camp, the release of
the fieldtrip inspired one person to set loose a flood of
jokes, all of which revolved around the theme of erection.
For example, he recounted, President Sukarno was at a banquet
of world leaders, each of whom exhibited some national prize
—Sputnik from Russia, the crown from England, and so on. When
Sukarno's turn came, he had no material prize but simply
exhibited his potency while shouting the phrase of the current ideology, "The new emerging force!"

The Fieldtrip

This began on the last day of the conference with a convoy of automobiles commandeered to carry everyone on a tour of Klaten.

At 009 hours, we visited the "Operations Room" of the office of the head of the region. After an inaudible welcome by a pretty secretary, the head, an engineer by profession who is a Muhammadijan, had an assistant roll down a huge wall map with flashing lights to show the location of projects in Klaten: dams, roads, improved farms. The aide then pushed a button to roll down a plastic overlay which showed sites of planned factories. The engineer also mentioned the building of 550 mosques. After the secretary's inaudible closing speech, we embarked on a tour.

First stop was a Muhammadijah high school, a visit which resembled in its pomp and circumstance typical public cele-brations in Java. Despite the billing as "sight-seeing," we were shown nothing, instead we were seated in a special sec-tion for honored guests in an assembly room where teachers and pupils had long been waiting. After a ceremonious distri-bution of snacks, there were two hours of speeches, which placed the convoy late for a meeting with a subdistrict offi-cer. Nevertheless, we stopped en route to see the counter-part to the high school, a Muhammadijah religious school for girls. These cowled and cloaked students had posted achieve-ment-oriented posters bearing such slogans as "No sweet with-out sweat" and "Shoot for the stars."

After being addressed ceremonially by the subdistrict offi-cer, we toured a model village, and heard more about new roads and schools which were said to represent REPELITA, the national development plan applauded by Muhammdijah at the Congress of 1968.

Visiting an umbrella factory manned by what the Darol Arqom participants termed "our people" (Muhammadijans), we enjoyed yet another reception in a reception room as big as the work-room. Then we saw workmen making umbrella handles. Nearby we saw a new dam, and in passing glimpsed other evidence of development. Late that afternoon we returned to camp to pre-pare for the closing ceremony.

Closing Ceremony

This final gathering was held in the large hall where par-ticipants had been sleeping since the opening ceremony. Mats were replaced with chairs. One side was reserved for the sarong and scarf clad women of 'Aisjijah, the other for male guests. Most camp leaders wore dark suits and ties (plus in some cases, dark glasses) and a few wore uniforms of the tan type sported by even nonmilitary people. This evening's agenda is outlined: The *Bema Wahju ilahi* (Qur'anic chant); opening speeches; speeches by the master of training; by a member; major speech; socializing; and close.

The major speaker, a certain military general, walks in, and everyone stands.

The ceremony is opened with the Qur'anic chant, then all sing the Indonesian national anthem.

Ibnu Salni, a middle-aged man from Solo who as a "Master" has overseen the proceedings, congratulates the 38 participants: all have passed the test.

Drs. Badruzzah, principle of the school, speaks of the participants' sacrifice in leaving their families, and he presents a diploma to the representative of the group, the oldest male. The general leads applause.

The representative of the participants now makes an eloquent and flowery speech, saying that indeed they have thought of their families (response: laughter; this gets at the Javanese concept of *kangen* - yearning for home). He jokes that this training camp was more than perfect—some trainees even had two pillows. "We shall sin badly if we do not go forth and do evangelism. We ask forgiveness for all our errors from James Peacock whom we accepted as a true participant."

A civil servant reads from a text given him by the head of the district (the Klaten engineer) who, he says, could not attend as he was just called to Djakarta by the President. It says that before the 1965 purge of Communism, Klaten could not develop, but after that it could owing to belief in the current national leader.

Now the rather stout and pompous general steps to the podium. An aide picks up his spectacles and lecture notes, places them on the podium, then steps behind it and stands in readiness throughout the speech. The general gives the Muslim greeting, then says he wants to take the opportunity to talk about religion and the search for truth.

There is danger in any one faction feeling that *it* is truth; is the Communist or the freethinker true?

Everything has its own rule for use—glasses can be worn only one place, on the face. Auto, train, Chevrolet, Mercedes, each of these must be used according to its rules.

Now man has his own rules, and they come from *his* maker: Allah! (Response: applause).

If you don't follow these, you suffer. Now I've made a chart...(two aides hang it up and give him a pointer stick) that shows religion from the holy book.

Tauhid (Unity of God) is blue. *Achlak* (ethics) is red, for its function is to control the emotions and desire (*nafsu*) which are false because they lack constancy. *Ibadat* (pious action) is purple. *Ilmu* (knowledge) is green.

Now all of these have their use. You can't kill emotion, for if you do you kill man. Like fire you must keep it under control, and then it can even be used to run a rocket.

Now (he shakes his stick at the audience), all comes from Muhammad—*Tauhid, Ibadat, Ilmu.* Follow him. *Ibadat* gives us Muslim identity. *Ilmu* lets you know when you properly conform to *Tauhid* and *Achlak.*

There's nothing bad in the world; even poison is good if used in the hospital. But false leadership can bedazzle, like shining gold false teeth (he smiles, showing his). NASAKOM is bull (*bohong*)! Anyone who follows the "old order" (Sukarnoist-Communist) is a fool.

All religions have these basic elements, only some are more complete than others. Christianity is weak in *ilmu*; it only got as far as elementary school. Prophet Jesus was not yet fully educated, whereas Muhammad had already graduated. And in Buddhism—forgive me for saying this—there is much *Tauhid* and *Achlak* but little *Ilmu.*

In sum, the message is to keep a balance, as in Islam.

We Indonesians can't imitate Japan; we have to follow the Muslim way: cooperate harmoniously. If you follow all this, you will be *sla-met* (safe and saved)!

No-o-o-ow, brothers (smiling): Let Islam be your guide.

I ask your forgiveness if I was crude; though the method was crude, the aim was spiritual. (Applause and everyone goes to bed.)

Next morning, June 16, at 5 A.M., most of us piled our bags in pedicabs and walked to Klaten to catch buses home.

Themes

During the fifteen days of Darol Arqom, idiosyncratic attitudes and reflections were expressed in the personal introductions, questions, and criticism of individual participants. Yet these individual expressions were woven into the collective process composed of lectures, ceremonies, and fieldtrip led by instructors, masters, and national figures elected and revered by the participants. This total experience of Darol Arqom reflects, in microcosm and intensely, themes fundamental to the Muhammadijah movement as a whole.

The central position in Muhammadijah consciousness of the belief in the oneness of God (*Tauhid*) is signified by the placing of this topic first on the lecture agenda. Malik's lectures on *Tauhid* echo the general Malayo-Muslim theme that the world is spiritual energy which can be either concentra-

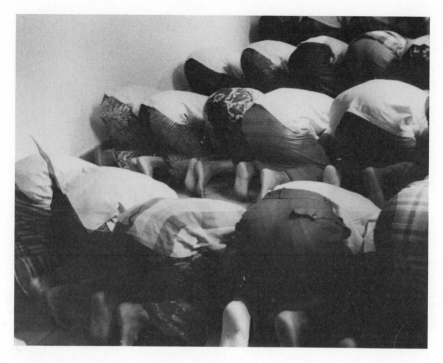

Plate 17:   Prayer at Darol Arqom.

ted in the one God or dissipated among the many forms, such
as shrines, charms, spirits, fetishes, and multiple gods.
Opposition between *Tauhid* and pantheism or polytheism was
much in participants' awareness; note their muttering of
"tsk, tsk" when Azhar described the fetishes of Iraq. (I
once overheard, as I was falling asleep one night, discussion
of my alleged belief in the polytheistic Trinity, owing to
my assumed affiliation with Western Christianity.) A survey
of participants' attitudes underlined the strength of their
classical reformist concern with unity or *Tauhid* versus the
pantheistic, polytheistic, and animistic features of syncretism (see Peacock, 1978).

The final lecture, that of the general, as well as the first
by Malik, made a linkage between syncretism and animal desire
(*hawa nafsu*), in opposition to *Tauhid* and its ethical deriva-
tive, *Achlak*. Distilled spirit, *Tauhid*, is contrasted to sensuous engagement and expression, whether with the animistic
spirits or the animalistic lust. *Achlak*, or ethics, together
with *Ilmu*, knowledge, control these earthy drives. An interesting contrast is apparent between the Islamic view of self,

as expressed by the general, and the syncretist, Hinduist
ones as expressed in such teaching as Jogjakarta's mystic
cult Pangestu. I have heard a Pangestu teacher expound a
chart much like the general's, similarly using colors to represent aspects of the self (black is desire and white is
spirituality). But where the Pangestu teacher literally
opposed black to white, as desire and spirituality, the general saw these elements as composing a continuum, along a
spectrum (red, green, blue). And where the Pangestu teacher
reflected a Hinduist super-spirituality in speaking of the
black desire as entirely destructive ("It will explode a
bomb," he said.), the general conceives that desire can be
harnessed ("It can fire a rocket."). The Muslims would seem
to express a more instrumentalist relation between desire
and spirituality, a sense that the one can serve the other;
the syncretist, a Hinduist super-spirituality that denies
natural desire altogether.

Nafsu, or desire, clearly concerned the participants, especially as the days wore on in the ascetic, one-sex camp; it
came out, finally, in jokes which concerned the phallus:
Sukarno's new emerging force. I have not heard this rather
Western-style joke among the syncretists, nor are they reported by other observers, so far as I know. The jokes may
reflect a reformist and Islamic conception of relation between
the spiritual and the natural, which contrasts with the
Hinduized syncretism.

Notably little mention was given to a triad of forms central
to Islam in general: Muhammad, the Qur'an, and the Pilgrimage.
The reason would seem to lie in distinctive emphases of the
Muhammadijan movement. Muhammad, Qur'an, and Pilgrimage are
concrete, sensory forms: the holy person, the holy book, and
a holy rite. For the Muhammadijan, concrete, sensory form
is replaced by abstract goals and organization. Thus, great
emphasis is given to *Djihad, Perdjuangan,* and *Da'wah*—collective
struggle and evangelism for the sake of the movement. These
emphases on collective, evangelistic struggle are reflected
in the Personal Introductions, as participants recount their
devotion to the movement, their role in a sometimes paramilitary battle to defend it, and the use of struggle as a category of organizing the life history and life quest; in the
lectures outlining principles of the Muhammadijah; in diagrams
chalking this movement as literally an arrow; in the hot issue of politicization which follows naturally from efforts at
collective organization; and in the militaristic air of the
camp, climaxed by the appearance of an army general.

Despite the emphasis on devotion to the movement, a striking
lack in the Personal Introductions is any account of emotional conversion to it; in many movements, including Christianity,
visions and other dramatic subjective conversion experiences

are recounted in testimonies. The Darol Arqom participants give testimonies that are quite strong and sometimes poignant. They tell of nonreformist backgrounds (traditionalist or N.U., syncretist or Hinduist, even P.K.I. or Communist families and villages), then report their conversion to Muhammadijah, a statement which is occasionally applauded with the response, "Praise be to God." Yet no one relates a vision or other emotional experience that stimulated this conversion. Here is no Paul on the road to Damascus, Luther on the way to his monastery, Muhammad in the Cave of Hira, or any of the similar experiences of movements. The lack of emotional conversion is general in the Muhammadijah, indeed throughout Southeast Asian reformist Islam. It appears to reflect a distinctively reformist Muslim conception of man; he is not born in original sin, from which he must convert by a dramatic wrench, but rather he is born good and he should steadily and systematically increase his commitment to the ethical norms laws of Islam (*Achlak*) by careful study of the scripture, performance of the rites, schooling in the belief, and struggle for the movement. The image of conversion is more rationalistic and legalistic than dramatistic, and remnants of an old Javanese view remain, as in the idea (expressed in the opening ceremony) that the struggle itself is not one of tension and turmoil, but of *sabar* (patience) and *ichlas* (stoic dedication), terminologies applied, we recall, by the biographers of K. H. A. Dahlan himself.

Though the Darol Arqom participants faithfully kept the prayers, and they devoted considerable discussion to purification by rite, there was some criticism of old-fashioned, irrational reverence for the sacred (note *Pak* A. R.'s joke about acting like the old sacral Muslim teachers, by putting a towel around the head). Emphasis was on analytical principles on the one hand, practical application on the other. Ritual expression of theology is less dominant than in traditionalist circles, which is a general tenet of reformism. The practicality is brought home at the end by the fieldtrip, where an engineer displays a map of projects including dams, villages, schools, factories, and, of course, mosques. These are then observed, though not without a certain degree of the traditional Javanese ceremonialism along the way. In the end, the practical and the spiritual are combined by having the man of affairs, the general, give his lecture on the ethics of Islam.

CHAPTER SEVEN

Muhammadijah

This study began by depicting the background of Southeast Asian Muslim reformism—the history and conditions of society and culture that gave rise to the movement. We then proceeded to characterize the origins, development, and contemporary existence of the largest and most viable Southeast Asian Muslim reformist organization, the Muhammadijah of Indonesia. Muhammadijah will be considered now in the context of the Indonesian society and culture, which is the stage on which it has thus far played its role.

As has been noted, a variety of Indonesian movements have been born since the beginning of the twentieth century. Most are now extinct. Several major movements were established almost simultaneously with Muhammadijah, for example, the nationalist Budi Utomo and Sarekat Islam. Other movements were founded within the next one or two decades, for example, the Indonesian Communist Party (P.K.I.), the Indonesian Nationalist Party (P.N.I.), and the conservative Muslim Party (N.U.), as well as many smaller organizations. Only the conservative and the reformist Muslim organizations, N.U. and Muhammadijah, still endure as viable entities. Explanation of the survival of N.U. lies partially in the strength of its grass-roots organization, which utilizes loyalties and networks of village Islam. The survival of Muhammadijah is likewise due to the strength of a grass-roots Islamic community, but in a more urban context. Muhammadijah's abstention from politics is doubtless also a factor.

Muhammadijah has done more than survive. It has flourished steadily, increasing its membership, expanding its organization until it now covers the entire span of the Indonesian islands stretching some three thousand miles from "Sabang to Merauke" (northern Sumatra to western New Guinea). Among the indigenous movements of Indonesia, whether nationalist, Communist, or Muslim, only Muhammadijah has built an extensive system of schools, hospitals, and social-welfare facilities. Throughout its efforts, spanning more than a half-century, Muhammadijah has a record of balanced budgets, efficient organization, and uncorrupted and dedicated leadership that cannot be matched by any of the other major movements of Indonesia or, for that matter, by many modernizing movements elsewhere. These achievements are only those most tangible, what is known as the *djasmane*; impressive, too, are those of the spirit or *rohane*.

Recognizing the great accomplishments of Muhammadijah, we must also delineate clearly the limits of its impact. A first boundary is geographic; with the exception of a small and loosely affiliated branch in Singapore, Muhammadijah has not yet extended outside Indonesia. A second and more important boundary is cultural; Muhammadijah has not converted the value system of the entire Indonesia nation to reformist Islam but has remained one of several important value systems or ideological streams within this pluralistic culture and society.

These value systems are most simply identified by the late President Sukarno's phrase NASAKOM, which refers to the nationalist, religious (Muslim), and Communist streams already mentioned. More complexly, this integrative triad is crosscut by hundreds of ethnic, regional, and tribal cultures. While at one time, some Indonesian Muslims aspired toward an Islamic state that would subsume all ethnicities, override such political divisions as the nationalist and the Communist, and guide all affairs in life, few seriously entertain such a vision today. At best, the devout aspire toward a unified Islamic nation in the strictly religious spheres such as ritual. To this end, the Muslims dominate the national Ministry of Religion whose status, roughly equal to that of the Indonesian State Department, reflects the great importance of religion in this society. Yet only a minority of Indonesians are fully practicing Muslims in the sense of faithfully doing the fast and pilgrimage, paying the religious tax, regularly praying at the mosque, and deriving their dominant ethical code through the study of the Qur'an and other Islamic teachings. While Islam has subtly pervaded many realms of Indonesian culture, for all Indonesians but the *santri* purists, the guiding value-system is a syncretic convergence of numerous streams of which reformist Islam is only one.

With some hesitation, one could compare this situation to that in the Protestant societies of the West. On the whole, it appears that the Muslim reformation in Southeast Asia has

been less pervasive than the Christian reformation in Europe
in structuring the value system of entire societies, especially if Protestantism is taken in the broad sense of the
Protestant Ethic which denotes a system of values that is
influential in societies such as England or America even among
non-Protestants such as Catholics or Jews; such an extent of
influence is not apparent for reformist Islam in Indonesia.
If this assessment is true, several explanations can be suggested. One is that Protestantism enjoyed the opportunity
during its early history to spread prior to the florescence
of the major secular forces of change, such as nationalism
and Communism. The Islamic reformation was denied this opportunity; Muhammadijah was founded almost simultaneously with
the major nationalist and Communist movements of Indonesia
and had to compete with them from the start. A second explanation is that Protestantism emerged in a society monolithically dominated by Christianity so that its reforms could
take hold within a ready-made, society-wide framework; the
Indonesian Islamic reformation did not occur in a society so
monolithically dominated by Islam.

   Whatever the explanation, it remains true that Muhammadijah
dominates the values of a restricted though important segment
of the Indonesian society. This segment is what we have
termed *santri*, the pious, active, committed Muslims who stand
in opposition to the less Islamized. These less Islamized
persons are in part denoted by such labels as nationalist and
Communist, which apply to the political realm. Beneath the
political, one may distinguish two dominant streams opposing
Islam: traditionalist and secularist. Traditionalism refers
to devotion to animistic custom, whether regional, ethnic, or
tribal; such custom is opposed to Islam at many levels, but
most fundamentally because of the violation of *Tauhid*.
Whether expressed through worship of the Jogjakarta god-king
or the Minangkabau rice-spirits, animism implies devotion to
differentiated rather than concentrated spirituality; in
animism, spirit is dispersed among multiple forms rather than
unified in that which is formless, known as Allah. Even
nationalism has been criticized by the *santri* in this light,
since it diverts allegiance from God to nation, sacralized as
a spiritualized territorial form such as Motherland. Secularism, too, implies a diverting of allegiance from God. The
new idols vary from the hedonistic ones that satisfy the *hawa
nafsu* (lust) of Djakarta's gambling, dancing, fornicating,
and luxury-seeking jet set, to the technological ones of the
Western-educated civilian or military bureaucrats. As many
observers have noted, Indonesian secularism and traditionalism
frequently flourish within the same individual: witness the
popularity of mystical meditation among urban technocrats.
For Muslim reformists, both traditionalism and secularism

violate Islam; conversely, for traditionalists and secularists, Islam stifles deeply-rooted or new-found identities. Accordingly, reformism holds only among the pious *santri*.

Within this group of pious *santri*, one must distinguish further between reformists and conservatives. The conservatives, exemplified by N.U., are not in all respects more conservative than the reformists. But they do retain more devotion to pre-reformation practices such as Sufi mysticism, worship of religious teachers, and adherence to the schools of law of medieval Islamic scholasticism. They also tend to be rural and agrarian, compared to the urban and commercial reformists. And they find reformism too pragmatic, too rationalistic, and too bureaucratic to satisfy their needs for spirituality and community.

What, then, does Muhammadijah mean for those Muslims who are its adherents? The meanings vary, of course, depending on the individual and circumstances. Yet one can delineate certain conditions that all Muhammadijans have experienced, and Muhammadijah can be interpreted as a response to these.

Social, economic, and political conditions in Indonesia have been turbulent and chaotic as part of the rapid changes occurring during the existence of Muhammadijah. During this three-quarters of a century, the touted *rust en orde* (quiet and order) of paternalistic Dutch Colonialism has been shattered by the *sturm und drang* of rebellion, revolution, and volatile independence. The nationalist struggles, followed by a harsh Japanese occupation, then years of revolutionary warfare, finally brought independence, but not stability. Under Sukarno, Indonesia experienced a successsion of toppled cabinets, civil war, then the chaotic Guided Democracy climaxed by the massacre of hundreds of thousands during the purge of Communism. Undercut by population explosion, the economy has sometimes verged on collapse. Inflation has accelerated, at times, at a rate difficult for a Westerner to imagine in terms of his recent experience. (Parallels can be found, perhaps, in the situation of Germany just before the rise of Hitler, and, for Americans, in the state of the Confederate economy during the last days of our Civil War.) As conditions deteriorated in the countryside, millions fled to the cities, only to find unemployment, vice, crime, and life in shantytowns. For the small businesspeople who form the backbone of Muhammadijah, these conditions of economic chaos—which reached their climax under Sukarno and have been heroically though only partially corrected under Suharto—posed great difficulty. A simple bureaucratic procedure or even a telephone call required a bribe, transport prices could triple overnight while currency would be devalued as quickly by 99 percent, and the ruling political forces were not sympathetic to the needs of business. For

the civil servant—all but the most exalted or corrupt—life
was a nightmare of trying to feed a family on a monthly salary
adequate to purchase only a few days' food, while trying to
carry out duties in a bloated, disorganized bureaucratic
structure. The Indonesian student faced not only the poverty
that besets students everywhere, but he must wonder also
whether the hard-pressed system would survive to grant a degree. And if he did manage to finish, he could anticipate
either unemployment or underemployment as an impoverished
civil servant. A 50 percent divorce rate undercuts the abil-
ity of the family to serve as a secure backup in times when
the larger society falters, and such substitutes for family
benevolence as insurance and welfare barely exist.

   Culturally, the Indonesian scene has long been a mixture
only partially blended. The animistic base, richly varied
among the several thousand islands, has never been completely
absorbed by any of the world religions—Hinduism, Confucianism,
Buddhism, Islam, or Christianity—which have penetrated this
so-called crossroads of culture. The looseness of the syncretism that has tied these elements together is demonstrated by
the periodic hiving off and intensification of one or the
other of them—the Islamic purification movement at the turn
of the century, the Hindu and Buddhist revivals today. Con-
frontation among the different faiths is usually localized,
as in spiritual contexts when one leader struggles to counter-
act the alleged sorcery of another, but it has occasionally
erupted into wide-scale conflict, of which the Gestapu massacre is the worst case in this century. To this already-
volatile mix of religious persuasions has been added the
various cultures and ideologies of the West. Initially
filtered by Dutch education, Western culture in Indonesia
now includes asphalt-jungle-style hoodlums, rock 'n' roll
singing and dancing, and the seamier sides of capitalistic
hedonism (such as X-rated movies). Major Western-based
movements—nationalism, socialism, Communism—have also been
grafted onto the weakening tissue of the indigenous tradition.

   What these circumstances mean to those experiencing them is
not simply stated. For the Westerner, conditioned by a system of values that glorifies rationality, efficiency, and
single-minded devotion to a goal-oriented faith, the social
and cultural existence of the modern Indonesian will seem
unbearably chaotic and directionless. Indonesians see things
a bit differently, since they have absorbed a culture that
values inner calm amid outer confusion and affirms harmony
among viewpoints which, to the Westerner, appear contradic-
tory. Yet one should not stereotype Indonesians as tranquil
Asians whose spiritual shell is impervious to outer shock.
Indonesians have revealed in many forms that they do experi-

ence certain kinds of trauma and disorientation in response to their modern social and cultural circumstances.

To begin with the most obvious condition, the economic, anyone in touch with ordinary people during the Sukarno times could hear them worry aloud about how to survive, and a Javanese psychiatrist remarked to me then that one of the most frequent fears his middle-class patients confided to him was simply that of economic catastrophe. In politics, worry about the society and government were expressed in hopes for a so-called "just prince," a charismatic figure who would swoop in and make all things right, and Sukarno himself was sacralized by many as just such a figure. Culturally, Indonesian literature has been one of the most sensitive expressions of anguish concerning conflict. Thus, in early twentieth-century novels, Indonesian authors frequently portrayed the struggle of characters to combine values of tradition and the West—a plot that usually ended in failure and tragedy. Evidence of personal concern with conflicting cultural tradition values is expressed in the Personal Introductions of the Darol Arqom, and in more private settings I have heard Indonesian students describe the concern they felt to somehow forge a "right way" out of the myriad faiths of their culture, many of which might be represented as conflicts within their own family.

What has Muhammadijah to offer the Indonesian who experiences in these ways a social and cultural disorder? Muhammadijah offers order. For the businessperson despairing of a rational system within which to make plans, Muhammadijah organizes cooperatives and other efforts at regularizing enterprise. For the teacher and student, Muhammadijah provides a rather well-run school system—limited in resources, to be sure, but rationally organizing those it has. Perhaps even more important than these real services, Muhammadijah provides a model. Here, in a society plagued by disorganization, Muhammadijah demonstrates the viability of an ideal of rationality, efficiency, honesty, and accomplishment. Puritan-like characters in Indonesia may despair of instituting their values of order and achievement in the wider society, but within the confines of the Muhammadijah, to some extent they succeed.

Culturally, Muhammadijah offers an alternative to the rich but confusing mixture of folk beliefs and great religions known as syncretism. Muhammadijah, as a distillation of Islam, provides a single authoritative text, a clear and formalized guide to conduct, and single, all-powerful God.

To claim that Muhammadijah has instituted order is not to deny that it has instigated change. After all, Muhammadijah is essentially a reform movement; it reforms. Muhammadijah has transformed schools from the *pesantren* type to the *madrasah* and the Western style. It has modernized secular

life by organizing cooperatives, hospitals, and welfare agen-
cies. It has helped to democratize manners and language. It
has liberated women by providing them a means to actively organize their own lives. It has purified religious practices
and beliefs.

Yet in its innovation, Muhmmadijah has remained within a
solid and stable tradition. That tradition is a faith believed to be an eternal, codified in a sacred scripture.
Whatever rationalization Muhammadijah has achieved affirms an
order which derives from a belief rooted in a fundamentalistic
trust in a sacral form: the holy scripture, which is the
revelation of Allah.

Bibliography

Abdullah, Taufik
    1971   *Schools and Politics: The Kaum Muda Movement in West Sumatra (1927-1933)*. Ithaca, N.Y.: Cornell University Modern Indonesia Project.

Alfian
    1970   "Modernism in Indonesian Politics: The Muhammadijan Movement during the Dutch Colonial Period, 1912-1942." Ph.D. thesis, University of Wisconsin, Madison.

Ali, A. Mukti
    1957   "The Muhammadijah Movement: A Bibliographical Introduction." M.A. thesis, McGill University, Montreal.

Anis, H. M. Junus
    1962   *Riwajat Hidup K. H. A. Dahlan, Dan Perdjoangannja*. Jogjakarta: Pimpinan Pusat Muhammadijah.

Bakker, D.
    1970   "Da'wah: Missionaire Mobilisatie van de Islam in Indonesia." *De Heerbaan* 3:220-247.

Bakker, F. L. O.
    1925   "De Opleving van den Islam in Djokdja." *De Macedonier* 29:161-178.

Erikson, Erik
    1958   *Young Man Luther: A Study in Psychoanalysis and History*. New York: Norton.

Mailrapport
          Reports from Departmen van Kolonien, Ministerie van Binnenlandse Zaken.

    1913   1096/13 Moehammadijah, Jogjakarta.

    1914   1782/14 Moehammadijah, Jogjakarta.

    1922   195x/22 Moehammadijah, Jogjakarta.

    1924   664x/24 Verslag der Jaarvergardering van de Vereeniging Moehammadijah, Jogjakarta.

1925a   672x/25   Moehammadijah-onderwijs-inrichtingen te
         Djokjakarta.

1925b   644x/25   Verslag van March 1925 Jogjakarta
         Congres Moehammadijah.

Moehammadijah
    1923   *Verslag "Moehammadijah" di Hindia Timoer Tahoen
            Ke X.* Januari-Desember.

Noer, Deliar
    1973   *The Modernist Muslim Movement in Indonesia 1900-
            1942.* London: Oxford University Press.

Peacock, James L.
    1973   *Indonesia: An Anthropological Perspective.*
            Pacific Palisades: Goodyear.

    1978   *Muslim Puritans: Reformist Psychology in
            Southeast Asian Islam.* Berkeley: University
            of California Press.

Pijper, G. F.
    1934   *Fragmenta Islamica: Studien Ober het Islamisme
            in Nederlandsche-Indië.* Leiden: Brill.

Salam, Solichin
    1963   *K. H. Ahmad Dahlan, Reformer Islam Indonesia.*
            Djakarta: Djajamurni.

    1965   *Muhammadijah dan Kabangunan Islam di Indonesia.*
            Djakarta: N.V. Mega.

Selosoemardjan
    1962   *Social Changes in Jogjakarta.* Ithaca, N.Y.:
            Cornell University Press.

Weber, Max
    1947   *The Theory of Social and Economic Organization.*
            Translated by T. Parsons and A. M. Henderson.
            New York: Oxford University Press.

    1958   *The Protestant Ethic and the Spirit of Capital-
            ism.* Translated by T. Parsons. New York:
            Scribners.

    1964   *The Sociology of Religion.* Translated by E.
            Fischer. Boston: Beacon Press.

Suggested Readings

Benda, Harry J.
    1958   *The Crescent and the Rising Sun: Indonesian Islam under the Japanese Occupation, 1942-1945.* The Hague: van Hoeve.

    1970   *South-East Asian Islam in the Twentieth Century.* In *The Cambridge History of Islam,* P. M. Holt, Ann K. S. Lambton, and Bernard Lewis, eds. Cambridge: Cambridge University Press, pp. 182-208.

Boland, B. J.
    1971   *The Struggle of Islam in Modern Indonesia.* The Hague: Martinus Nijhoff.

Castles, Lance
    1967   *Religion, Politics, and Economic Behavior in Java: The Kudus Cigarette Industry.* New Haven: Yale University Southeast Asian Studies.

Drewes, G. W. J.
    1955   *Indonesia: Mysticism and Activism.* In *Unity and Variety in Muslim Civilization,* G. E. von Grunebaum, ed. Chicago: University of Chicago Press, pp. 284-310.

Federspiel, Howard M.
    1970   "The Muhammadijah: A Study of an Orthodox Islamic Movement in Indonesia." *Indonesia* 10:57-80.

Geertz, Clifford
    1960   *The Religion of Java.* Glencoe, Ill.: Free Press.

    1968   *Islam Observed: Religious Development in Morocco and Indonesia.* New Haven: Yale University Press.

Mukti, Ali
    1965   "Modern Islamic Thought in Indonesia." *Islamic Review* 53:23-27.

Samson, Allan A.
    1968   "Islam in Indonesian Politics." *Asian Survey* 8:1001-1017.

Siegel, J. T.
    1969   *The Rope of God.* Berkeley: University of California Press.

Wertheim, W. F.
    1965   *East-West Parallels: Sociological Approaches to Modern Asia.* Chicago: Quadrangle.

Glossary

abangan - Hindu-Buddhist-animist (syncretist) Muslim

achlak - ethics

agama - religion

agama perbandingan - comparative religion

akal - rationality

chatib - religious official

da'wah - evangelism

hadji - Muslim who made the pilgrimage to Mecca

ibadat - pious action

ichlas - stoic

idjtihad - interpretation of scripture analytically

ilmu - knowledge

kijai - Islamic teacher

madrasah - school combining Muslim and secular instruction

modin - village Muslim official

nafsu - desire

perdjuangan - struggle

sabar - patience

santri - purist Muslim

tabligh - Islamic meeting or sermon

Tauhid - Unity of God

Index